House Recycling

House Recycling
The Best Real Estate Opportunity for the '80s

Mary Weir

Contemporary Books, Inc.
Chicago

Library of Congress Cataloging in Publication Data

Weir, Mary, 1943–
　　House recycling.

　　Includes index.
　　1. Dwellings—Remodeling.　　2. Real estate investment.
I. Title.
HD1390.5.W44　　　1982　　　332.63′243　　　81-69617
ISBN 0-8092-5941-9　　　　　　　　　　　　　　AACR2

Copyright © 1982 by Mary Patterson Weir
All rights reserved
Published by Contemporary Books, Inc.
180 North Michigan Avenue, Chicago, Illinois 60601
Manufactured in the United States of America
Library of Congress Catalog Card Number: 81-69617
International Standard Book Number: 0-8092-5941-9

Published simultaneously in Canada by
Beaverbooks, Ltd.
150 Lesmill Road
Don Mills, Ontario M3B 2T5
Canada

Contents

Acknowledgments vii

The Weir Track Record, 1966 to 1980 viii

part I. You Can Make Money Recycling Houses in the 1980s xiii

1. Getting More Out of Life—Starting Now 1
2. How Recycling Makes You Richer in the 1980s 8
3. Needs and Neighborhoods of a Big Profit-Maker 16

part II. Getting the Most Out of a Good Situation 25

4. The Weir Fifty Percent Rule: Sure-Fire Recycles 27
5. Finding a Bank Mortgage for Your 1980s Inflation-Beater 35

6. Completing the Financing and Closing the Recycle Deal   *45*

part III. Clearing the Way for Recycling the Profitable House   **57**

7. Making a Recycle Plan That Pays Off in the 1980s   *59*
8. Blazing a Paper Trail for Fast Recycling   *69*
9. Being Your Own Contractor to Build Up Recycle Profit   *78*
10. Tools for Fun and Profit in the 1980s Recycle   *84*

part IV. Maximizing Profit on the All-Important House Systems   **91**

11. Inexpensive Insulation for Maximum Energy Savings   *93*
12. Making Plumbing Pay Off in the 1980s Recycle   *100*
13. Modern Heating for the Inflationary 1980s   *107*
14. Modern Electrical Service for the Profitable Recycle   *114*

part V. Giving Your Recycle Maximum Selling Power   **121**

15. Exteriors to Bring Prospects in Off the Street   *123*
16. Recycling Interiors to Create Fabulous Bargains   *129*
17. Finding a Mortgage for Your Full-Price Buyer   *138*
18. Intelligent Selling to Maximize the Recycle Profit   *143*

Index   **149**

Acknowledgments

This is to acknowledge the enormous contribution and pioneering of Sam Weir: there is no fundamental part of the recycling process that was not worked out in partnership with him. And secondly, I want to acknowledge the work of Morten Lund, the professional writer who persevered and put together this book, as he did the previous book, through the inevitable ups and downs of book authorship and publication.

THE WEIR TRACK RECORD
1966 TO 1980

House No.	House Location	Year Purchased	Purchase Price
1	18 Beach St.	1966	4,500
2	265 New Ocean Ave.	1968	17,000
3	32–32A Riverdale Ave.	1969	13,800
4	30 Shrewsbury Dr.	1970	20,000
5	5 Griffin St.	1970	15,300
6	1 Riverview Ave.	1971	8,000
7	12 Main St.	1971	11,300
8	Route 100, Vermont	1971	21,500
9	559 Manahasset	1971	24,500
10	78 Ocean Ave.	1972	26,500
11	Goldencrest	1972	45,000
12	71 Victor Ave.	1972	9,000
13	1–3 Ocean Ave.	1973	35,000
14	34 Washington Ave.	1973	26,500
15	5 Maplewood Ave.	1974	15,000
16	477 Ocean Ave.	1974	50,000
17	477-A Ocean Ave.	1974	25,000
18	91 Rumson Rd.	1974	80,000
19	The Lindens	1975	90,000
20	Linden Pond	1975	30,000
21	141-A Rumson Rd.	1975	30,000
22	57 Hathaway	1975	50,000
23	16 Locust Ave.	1976	11,700
24	18 Locust Ave.	1976	11,800
25	59 Sea View Ave. (Lot)	1976	—
26	Manhassett (Lot)	1976	—
27	10 Acres, Vermont	1976	12,000
28	114 Ocean Ave.	1976	20,000
29	114-A Ocean Ave.	1976	10,000
30	25-27-29 Monmouth Rd.	1977	44,000
31	11 Center St.	1978	37,500
32	19 Lafayette	1979	30,000

Misc. Expenses & Material Costs	Total Expenditure	Rental Profits	Selling Price or Value	Wages & Gross Profit	Equity: Wages & Net Profit
14,314	18,814	30,000	31,000	61,000	42,106
31,157	48,157	40,000	106,000	146,000	97,843
12,775	26,575	17,000	48,000	65,000	38,425
9,800	29,800	10,000	36,000	46,000	16,200
2,410	17,710	5,000	46,000	51,000	33,290
3,000	11,000	3,000	18,000	21,000	10,000
10,561	21,861	9,000	42,000	51,000	29,139
8,072	29,572	2,000	55,000	57,000	27,428
7,691	32,191	8,000	35,000	43,000	10,809
8,680	35,180	8,500	55,000	63,500	28,320
26,272	71,272	5,000	180,000	185,000	113,728
8,256	17,256	—	26,650	26,650	9,394
5,000	40,000	13,500	95,000	108,500	68,500
5,000	31,500	—	37,000	37,000	5,500
7,200	22,200	—	30,900	30,900	8,700
9,680	59,680	30,000	135,000	165,000	106,320
5,000	30,000	10,000	50,000	60,000	30,000
21,000	182,000	—	395,000	395,000	293,000
65,000	155,000	—	177,000	177,000	22,000
60,000	90,000	—	185,000	185,000	95,000
2,000	32,000	—	50,000	50,000	18,000
9,000	59,000	—	60,000	60,000	1,000
4,000	15,700	—	25,000	25,000	9,300
4,000	15,800	—	30,000	30,000	14,200
2,000	2,000	—	25,000	25,000	23,000
1,000	1,000	—	20,000	20,000	19,000
2,000	14,000	—	18,000	18,000	4,000
16,000	36,000	—	95,000	95,000	59,000
5,000	15,000	—	46,000	46,000	31,000
50,000	94,000	—	172,000	172,000	78,000
14,800	52,300	—	79,000	79,000	17,000
12,600	42,600	—	69,000	69,000	16,400
					1,375,602

House Recycling

part I

You Can Make Money Recycling Houses in the 1980s

1

Getting More Out of Life—Starting Now

Most of us would like to know how to get more out of life: more money, more security, more satisfaction. But it is not easy to know how to do that, or where to start. This book will show you a clear, direct path to that richer, more rewarding, more creative life—that is my promise.

Fifteen years ago, I bought my first house—a small shack for $4000—and "recycled" it. That first recycle started me on a great and rewarding path. Creatively and financially, recycling has enabled me to get what I most wanted in my life—reasonable control over my own destiny. By the end of 15 years, I had recycled over 30 houses, and had a net worth of a million dollars. Not bad, considering I started out with nothing except an idea and a wretched house.

You don't have to be a "lifetime" recycler, as I am, to reap the rewards of recycling. You can start out while holding down a regular five-day-a-week job. Recycling a *single* house can make anyone considerably richer. Pick any house using the rules set forth in this book, and it can take you less than a year to make your profit. All you invest is your spare time and a modest amount of money. The profit is sure—and amazing.

Making Dreams Come True

My first recycle was the house at 18 Beach Street in Rumson, New Jersey. Recycling turned this unprepossessing, deteriorated one-family dwelling into a completely renovated duplex. From there I went on to recycle much larger houses.

My eleventh recycle was Goldencrest, the first of three "mansion recycles." I took abandoned, dilapidated former architectural triumphs (one was a Stanford White design), and turned them into beautiful, viable homes. It gave me a feeling of deep personal accomplishment to return such houses to the community, and the work was creatively and financially satisfying—a characteristic of recycling.

Today, I am recycling a hundred-year-old Seabright, New Jersey, beachfront hotel, The Peninsula House. Turning it into a multimillion dollar entertainment complex is the most ambitious project I have ever undertaken. In its heyday, The Peninsula House had been a vacation retreat for the rich and famous, including actor Bert Lahr (the Cowardly Lion in *The Wizard of Oz*), comedian Jack Pearl, tennis champ Alice Marble, and author Robert Ruark. And there was a little fellow by the name of Frank Sinatra who wandered around on the beach with his parents.

The hotel was a bastion of high-level elegance in dining, service, and accommodations. It was impeccably Edwardian in style, an epitome of the good life in those days. But times changed, vacation styles changed, and the clientele dwindled. In 1959, The Peninsula House was boarded up and left to deteriorate. The only life remaining on the site was a seasonal beach club operation. This was the scene when I bought the property in 1979.

My plan—so far carried out successfully—has been to return

The Peninsula House to its former elegance while incorporating the changes necessary to ensure a profit. The Edwardian-style Peninsula House Restaurant opened in the spring of 1981, with both outdoor and indoor dining; the restaurant's lower-level wine-cellar dining room opened early in the summer of 1981. The opulent Peninsula House Lobby, a cocktail bar, and adjacent banquet hall, were ready to go in late summer of 1981. All this extensive restoration, renovation, and redesign took an enormous amount of money. Thanks to fifteen years of profitable recycling, I had more than enough money to make my most dramatic dream come true.

The Goal of Recycling

Recycling will help you realize your dreams, no matter what they are. You may not have as elaborate a dream as I had; you may not want to invest fifteen years recycling in order to accumulate the kind of capital that I have accumulated. That's fine. The point is that *whatever* your dream, recycling can make it possible. You *can* secure your future. You *can* build a financial reserve. You *can* make your life richer and more satisfying. The opportunity is out there for everyone.

The Heart of Recycling

First of all, you have to understand that recycling is very different from *redecorating* (as the word is commonly understood). The usual redecorator works on a cost-plus basis and has no responsibility for turning the project into a profitable commercial venture. Recycling is definitely aimed at making a profit.

Fifteen years ago, I had very limited resources; yet I made great changes in each house. I designed interiors and exteriors around "found objects" or around pieces that cost next to nothing. The outside stair on the first recycle, for instance, was built from driftwood slabs found right on the Seabright Beach.

Nothing in that first house was bought at wholesale; I bought everything at prices *less* than wholesale at flea markets, furniture auctions, and garage sales. The difference between the prices I paid and the prices typical of decorator supply stores was my profit.

The confusion between recycling and redecorating persists. People seek me out constantly to "learn about recycling." But few of them want to sit through auctions, sift merchandise at lawn sales or share in the sawing, sweeping, cleaning, scrubbing, spackling, and sanding, which are the minimum inescapable set of chores in a recycle. Most people want to *hire* labor to do those sorts of things. What they really want is to put on their designer clothes and go to a decorator showroom.

But the heart of recycling is a world away from shopping at decorator supply counters. *The heart of recycling is in continual, intense cost-cutting, and in picking up the hammer yourself.*

Take my first recycle at 18 Beach. Anybody could have done what I did by spending a pile of money; I did it with almost no money. In two years, I created something with nothing more than inspiration and small change. And at the end of two years, 18 Beach was remortgaged for a much higher sum than the original cost, and that money financed my second recycle. I was on my way to a million dollars. If *I* could do that—starting with no money and no training—so can you.

Commitment to Recycling

To recycle successfully, you do have to make a commitment. My first recycling work had to be fitted around the needs of my two children and housekeeping chores. My life was anything but easy—exciting, but not easy. Only a strong commitment kept me going.

In those first years, I had no social life to speak of. I rarely took weekends off. The recycling work went on day-in and day-out, week-in and week-out. My contemporaries were taking tennis lessons and going skiing, while I was buying at garage sales and stripping furniture. They became practiced skiers and tennis players. I achieved financial independence.

Recycling in the 1980s

Now let's shift subject for a while; let's consider recycling in this decade. This book extends, magnifies, and adds to the ideas presented in the book I coauthored in the 1970s, *How We Made A Million Dollars Recycling Great Old Houses*. Much new material in this current book specifically counters the unwarranted pessimism that has descended like a fog on real estate in the 1980s.

The "pessimists" have a doomsday speech that runs like this: "If you purchase a house, your mortgage rate is absolutely horrendous. The interest eats away *all* the eventual profit. And when you try to sell, your *buyers* are scared off by the same high interest rates. So you are left sitting on a house with the 'interest meter' running and no buyers. How can you make money on houses today?"

It is true that interest rates are higher, and that buyers are scarcer. But this is also true: *Recycling is a sure way around those 1980 problems.* In this book we shall see how.

This book focuses on a different kind of recycler than the first book. *How We Made A Million Dollars Recycling Great Old Houses* was written for "full-time recyclers," people who give up careers in other fields to become recyclers. This book is written for the "part-time recycler" who is going to do one or two houses. (Soon after the first book was published, I realized that most people would never want to give up their regular careers to become full-time recyclers; so I started making notes for this book.)

Looking at Investments

In the 1980s, more than ever, recycling houses provides a safe, sizable return on a modest investment, while other "good little investments" of the 1960s and 1970s are long gone.

What were those good little investments?

They were:

1. Buying a house to live in (home owning).

2. Buying a house to hold for resale—not to live in (speculation).
3. Building a savings account.
4. Buying stocks and mutual funds.
5. Buying money market fund and certificates of deposit.

How well do these work today? Let's look:

1. *Buying a home to live in (home owning).* Back in the 1960s you borrowed money at 5 to 8 percent, and the price of the house increased faster than prices in general. Since you lived in the house, you also profited because you did not have to pay any rent. This was a really good investment.

Let's take an example. You could buy a $45,000 house for $15,000 down and pay small monthly installments on a $30,000 mortgage. At the end of ten years, you would have paid out say $25,000 in interest, but the house would have doubled in value to $90,000. And that would constitute a nice contribution to your lifestyle. The house cost you $45,000, plus $25,000 interest, or $70,000 total. The current value of the house ($90,000) plus the amount saved in rent (say $30,000) equals $120,000. Subtract the cost of $70,000, and you have a $50,000 profit. Now subtract an average of five percent inflation per year, and your adjusted profit is $25,000—still a nice chunk.

What happens today?

It's hard to forecast what will happen in the next ten years in simple figures. But the mortgage that you will get today will likely be a variable mortgage whose rate varies with the current rate of interest. The interest may average out from 10 to 15 percent for the coming years. No one knows what will happen. That's the point.

Profit in home owning used to be predictable. The mortgage rate was fixed, and the rate of inflation was low. But today everything is fluctuating. You don't have any way of telling whether your home will be a good investment, or whether the combination of rising interest rate and high inflation will rob you of any chance to build a financial reserve. Further, home owning is getting to be less and less of a modest investment. You could pay $150,000 today for a house that ten years ago sold for

$45,000. You cannot count on traditional home owning as a source of profit on a modest investment.

Let's look at other kinds of investment.

2. *Buying a house for resale without improvement (speculation).* Here your situation is even less inviting because you're keeping the house on the market, not living in it; therefore you are not saving rent. Your hope is that the house will appreciate in value faster than all other prices will rise. That's just not happening often enough today to make speculation a good bet. In other words, speculating in real estate is far too risky for the small investor who cannot afford to see his savings dwindle.

3. *Savings accounts.* In the past decade some people put their money in interest-bearing accounts in savings banks or savings and loan associations. The banks were enticing new customers to open accounts with giveaway toasters. They turned out to be very expensive toasters. Savings accounts paid somewhere in the neighborhood of 7 to 8 percent over the past ten years while inflation averaged out at 10 to 12 percent. Every year, in comparison to prices, the amount in the account was relatively less. Not a good investment at all.

4. *Common stock.* A good investment even today for those who can buy a half million dollar portfolio and thus attract the attention of a reasonably sharp stock broker who can spend the time needed to make profitable trades. If you decide to play the market on your own, the statistics say that you lose, just as in roulette—and sometimes you lose rather quickly, too.

5. *Mutual funds.* In general they have not outperformed inflation in the past few years; the go-go years when there were plenty of good stocks to pick from are over.

6. *Money market fund and certificates of deposit.* These have been yielding rates equal to and sometimes better than inflation. But, on average, you come out even. It is "a wash," which means you have a good "hedge" against inflation, but are not building up any reserve.

So where do you go to make a profit and build a reserve? Recycling. It's the soundest modest investment you can make today. It can make you richer within the year. Read on.

2

How Recycling Makes You Richer in the 1980s

We've said that recycling works in today's difficult turbulent world. Now it's time to show *how* recycling guarantees a profit when home owning and speculation do not.

Recycling is a very short process: You buy the house, get in, make substantial improvements, raise the market value, and sell out—all within a short period of time. During that period you pay high interest on your mortgage, but so what? You've still got a built-in profit beyond all that. The way you picked the house, the way you fixed it up, and the price at which you can offer it—all guarantee profit. No need to hold a mortgage for years at a high interest rate. When you finish your recycle, it's ready to be sold. Even though you offer it at a bargain price, you still make a profit.

Let's take an example. You borrow $40,000 on a mortgage loan at 10 percent—a low interest rate by current standards. This means you pay out $4000 in interest during the year you recycle.

Now let's say that you pay a much higher interest rate of 15 percent; then, you pay out $6000 interest during the year, or $2000 more in interest. In the big recycling picture, where you have increased the value of the house by tens of thousands of dollars, the extra $2000 is not a critical increase. You still make money.

That takes care of the high-interest problem. Now what about the scarce-buyer problem? Sure, buyers are scarcer. And, because fewer people can afford houses today, there are more unsold houses on the market. But, recycling, as we shall see, is a way to buy a house for a low price, fix it up inexpensively, and market it—still at a bargain price. The recycler's house sells *first*. As long as there are any buyers at all, the recycled house will have buyers because it's the best buy around.

Let's look again at speculation and homeowning for comparison.

The speculator. These days he has bought in at a high price. He finds that, contrary to expectation, the price of the house is not rising faster than inflation. So he can either sell now and take a comparative loss, or he can hang on at high interest and hope that inflation will slack off, or house prices zoom. It's a terrible gamble. Speculating is risky; recycling is not.

The home-owner. Today he buys at current high prices and has to pay high interest. He saves by not paying rent, but he may end up with no "profit" after inflation when he sells the house. He kept *even* with inflation, but the recycler meantime has been *beating* inflation with an immediate large rise in the market value through quick, intelligent improvement. Only the recycler escapes the high-price/high-interest/scarce-buyer bind.

Convincing the Banks

When I first started out, there were two kinds of people profiting on houses. First, there were the home-owners—they would add renovations at a leisurely pace, with no aim at quick profit. Banks gladly loaned money to home-owners to finance their renovations.

Second, there were the speculators, who bought and sold houses like stocks and bonds, often holding them for less than a year. Banks do not lend money for speculation, and so the speculators had to find their own sources for any improvement money.

Only a very few people were recycling. Therefore, when I first asked a bank officer for a home-improvement loan to buy recycling materials for my second recycle, he said, "Sorry, we don't lend money for speculation."

Patiently, I explained that recycling was not speculative. It is a process ensuring a built-in profit because a relatively small amount of work adds up to a quick profitable rise in the house's market value.

The banker, brushing lint off his pin-striped lapel, said that as long as I was not living in the house, it was speculation. End of interview.

Later on, when I was five recycles down the line and had doubled the market value of the house on four out of five recycles, that same banker was *delighted* to lend me money for home improvement. I had convinced him that a recycle leads to sure profit.

Most banks today regard recycling as separate from speculation. Go to a bank with a sound recycling plan and they may well loan you improvement money on the spot. (A bank is in the business of loaning out money at interest. If you can convince the bank that you can easily pay its interest out of your profit, there's no problem.)

Recycling Rewards Judgment

A key ingredient to getting richer through recycling is good judgment in determining which home improvements to make.

Here is a very simple example. Let's say you own a house in a neighborhood where most of the houses of equivalent size sell for $90,000. These other houses, however, have two baths; your house has only one, and thus is worth only $80,000. So you spend about a month of your spare time, and $1000 in materials, to install a second bathroom. Now your house is worth $90,000, just like the other houses. Good judgment, some sweat, and $1000 in cash raised the value of your house $10,000, just like that.

Let's look at what can happen in a case of poor judgment.

A man owns a house worth $80,000 in a neighborhood where the other houses sell for $90,000; so, he figures that he'll put in a recreation room for $5000. But he has made a mistake. The reason that the other houses are worth $10,000 more is that they have a second bathroom. So, he spends $5000 on his recreation room, and then puts his house up for sale. Unfortuately, he realizes too late his house is *still* only worth $80,000. He has thrown his money away. A recreation room is a selling point, but it won't raise the price of a one-bathroom house up to that of a home with two bathrooms.

In other words, just putting in any old improvement won't increase market value. It may help you sell the house, but dollar-for-dollar there's no pay-off. If you want satisfactory profit on your materials investment, you have to add *profitable* improvements.

Houses that need a *number* of profitable improvements, I call "houses with profitable needs." Houses with the right combinations of profitable needs are houses *ripe* for recycle; often their market value can be *doubled* within a year.

And those houses are out there, believe me. But you have to go out and find them yourself. Only you can tell, after proper investigation, whether any houses in your town have the right combination of needs and the right locations (we will get to location in a minute). There is no way I can tell you long-distance whether or not there are "recyclable" houses in your town. (Yet people constantly write and telephone me to ask that very question.) You have to find *that* out for yourself.

The next logical question is: If there are all those potentially profitable houses out there in my town, why don't people rush out, buy them, and rake in that profit? Answer: It takes an educated eye to spot these potentially profitable, "recyclable" houses.

And that is one aim of this book: to sharpen your "eye," your perception, and judgment, so that when one of those houses comes on the market, you see *big opportunity*—where others see only a not-so-hot-looking house for sale. By the time you finish this book, you will *know* when you see a house that fits the recycle pattern.

Once you learn to recognize the pattern, you will *smell* a good recycle as soon as you step in the door. That gut reaction, of course, has to be checked out by "running the numbers" (figuring out the potential profit on paper). Otherwise, you can get fooled. But, most often that gut feeling is right. I know because I have made money on that gut feeling for years.

Recycling Has Many Payoffs

We've seen now how good judgment pays off in recycling. The time invested also pays off in recycling. If you invest in the stock market, there is not much you can do to boost your profit: prayer, perhaps. But, in recycling, you can contribute heavily to your profit by investing your own time and energy.

Say you buy a house for $50,000 and you spend $10,000 on labor to fix it up, plus $5000 in materials, and $15,000 for everything else (interest, insurance, taxes). Your costs are $80,000. You double the original market value and sell for $100,000. Your profit is $20,000. And you can raise your profit to $30,000 by doing the labor yourself. Not bad for a spare-time occupation.

Now, let's look at another way that recycling pays off.

Recycling pays off in tax advantages. When you work for a salary, you have no legitimate business deductions to speak of, since presumably your firm reimburses you for expenses the business necessitates. But, as a recycler, you can deduct things like car expenses (to some extent), depreciation on tools, depreciation of the house being recycled, and some of the mortgage or rent on your own house (if you use part of it as an office or recycle workshop).

Then, when you pull in a profit, that profit is taxed at the long-term capital gain rate (you've held the house a year)—a much lower rate than regular income tax. And, of course, you don't have to pay a tax on the increased value of the recycled house until you sell the house and actually take the profit. Even then, you can reinvest in another house and shelter the profit until that house is sold, and so on.

Then there is the *rental option*. You can rent the house for at least enough to pay for the cash outflow; thus, you can hang onto the house without it costing you a penny until you find an opportune time—in tax terms—to sell out.

Today, only three out of every ten Americans can afford to buy their own house. Inflation kicks the price of houses ever higher. But, when you buy a "recyclable house," you buy for much less than the potential market price; therefore, you can afford a house and make money besides.

Lastly, the recycler can save rent by living in the house while recycling it, even if this isn't the most comfortable kind of living. I can remember moving into houses that were terribly uncomfortable—installing space heaters and putting plastic sheets over broken windows, just so I could live in the house free while working on it. That way, the rent savings were part of my profit. (I always hated renting, because it gives money away that I could put to better use.)

Recycling Means Being Willing

To be a recycler and have the recycling advantages, you have to be *willing*. First, you have to be willing to learn. Second, you have to be willing to work.

What kinds of things do you have to be willing to learn? Well, you have to be willing to learn the basics of wiring, plumbing, heating, insulating, carpentry, and a good deal more to really make your profit. (One of my friends who contracted out all the work done on his house ended up with a *loss* rather than a profit.)

One recycle may require grouting tiles, laying brick, and removing a structural wall. The next recycle may require plumbing, insulating, wallpapering, and laying carpets. Whatever it is, you have to be ready to learn to do it.

None of the jobs required in recycling is out of reach of the average person. All you need is a willingness to learn from books, from professionals, and from trial and error. In other words, you have to be willing to go out and begin!

This book will give you the basic general framework, but, for a particular job such as replumbing, you have to ask questions of a plumber, talk to your local plumbing supply store, and read up on it in a plumbing manual. You have to learn what questions to ask and how to get the answers. I call this "the q. and a. way to profit."

In school, a poor teacher will often discourage questions by ridiculing anyone who asks a basic, or "naive" question. But, in life, you have to persist; you ask those naive questions and get your answers.

Let's say that you have never estimated the worth of a house, and you see one up for sale. How do you find out if it's potentially a bargain or not? Why not go out and ask a real estate agent? And after you talk to one agent, talk to another agent. Don't hurry it. You are learning. Ask a bank mortgage loan officer. His job requires him to know about real estate values.

Dirt and Fatigue Are Part of It

And now we come to the "willingness to work" part of it. My parents never understood what I saw in recycling. For one thing, a recycler gets all dirty. My parents did not raise their daughter to lug lumber, scrape floors, and mix cement. But once my recycling career led to my buying The Peninsula House, my parents began to see sense in recycling. And that is it: recycling calls for hard work, sometimes dirty work (you never finish the day looking like a debutante), but it rewards you by opening the door to getting *more* out of life. (The Peninsula House is a pretty impressive "more.")

If your idea of a perfect lifestyle is to spend your spare time playing tennis and going skiing, then recycling is not for you. But the recycler will find, as I did, that although tennis and skiing are fun, you get even more fun out of life by winning the financial game.

Recycling as a Positive Experience

On the psychological side, recycling is just what the doctor ordered. The best part of recycling is the satisfaction of *creating*.

What an ego boost it is to bring back to life a house that has suffered years of neglect! You are returning depleted housing stock to the community and adding to the total community wealth. You are a producer, not just a consumer.

The recycler is in control. He or she "makes it work" the way the frontier people did, with their heads and their hands. The recycler is not waiting around for the boss to give a raise and make life better. Being able to meet your own needs is a great feeling. Recycling can make you richer in many ways.

3

Needs and Neighborhoods of a Big Profit-Maker

There are nine steps to recycling:
1. Finding a house with the right needs in the right neighborhood. (We deal with finding a house in this chapter. The other steps will follow in subsequent chapters.)
2. Spotting Sure-Fire combinations and bidding low.
3. Getting an advantageous mortgage loan and other financing.
4. Closing the purchase conclusively and legally.
5. Making a detailed recycle plan to control costs.
6. Blazing a proper "paper trail" to ensure nonstop recycling.
7. Recycling the house systems (plumbing, heating, etc.).
8. Recycling the exterior, interiors, and landscaping.
9. Using selling know-how to get the highest possible sales price.

Looking for Houses with Simple Needs

Let's start out with Step 1: the idea of "needs." You are looking for a house that "needs" rehabilitating in specific ways. You are looking for a house that needs a second bathroom, not one that "needs" a cellar bar and ping-pong room. You are looking for a house with profitable needs to fill—there have to be *enough* of them. This requires weeks, not days, of looking.

Only *one* house in *fifty* has the right combination of "needs" that can be met cheaply enough to create a good profit. Step 1 of recycling is a careful search. A recycler who is not thorough enough at Step 1 soon becomes an ex-recycler.

A woman once told me that she had been searching unsuccessfully for "recyclable" houses in her home town. I was about to tell her she was probably being admirably choosy, but just to be sure, I said, "How many have you looked at?"

"Oh," she said, "four or five, at least."

She didn't quite have the idea.

The Needs Rule

The simpler the "needs," the better.

The ideal recycle is a house relatively easy to fix up; all its systems are pretty much intact with all the plumbing, insulating, and wiring in place. Recycling this house calls for mostly "elbow grease," rags, sponges, mops, and buckets of ammonia suds. This is a recycle that offers a "quick turnaround." It yields the biggest profit for the least time invested.

Now we come to the idea of "ladder of needs." Some needs are difficult and time-consuming to fill. These we call top-of-the-ladder needs. Others are bottom-of-the-ladder needs; these are quickly filled, but all the same make a considerable difference in the resale value.

What you are looking for most of all is a house with bottom-of-the-ladder needs. Then, second, you want the house to have some middle-of-the-ladder needs, which when filled, raise the price of the house considerably. Lastly, *one* top-of-the-ladder need, at most. Otherwise, you get in over your head.

Here is a partial "ladder of needs" starting with the typical easy jobs up to the difficult ones:

1. cleaning, spackling, painting
2. floor refinishing, wallpapering
3. modernizing kitchen, bath
4. removing interior walls
5. adding a bedroom in existing space
6. adding a bathroom in existing space
7. removing a structural wall
8. redoing plumbing
9. redoing insulation
10. reroofing, replacing siding
11. installing new heating system
12. adding new room in old space
13. adding new bathroom in old space
14. exterior redesign, separate buildings

The ladder of needs is an important concept; it can prevent "the slaughter of the innocents," or "the trap of the Handyman's Special."

If you have a "Handyman's Special," a house that has lots of top-of-the-ladder needs (numbers 8 through 14), turn it down. Too many complex, difficult, expensive tasks make cost estimates undependable. You can too easily lose your margin of profit. Just because you are "handy," don't go looking for tough problems. People who insist on getting into complicated renovations will finish, often as not, by becoming much handier and also much poorer.

Take two houses, each potentially worth $60,000 when fixed up, both for sale at $30,000. One house looks terrible—full of mildew, dirt, garbage, and junk in every room. But when you look closely, once you've got the mess cleaned up, all the house needs is varnish, wallpaper, curtains, and carpets. It is a "Cleaning Woman's Special." The second house is clean inside, and attractive, but it needs rewiring, replumbing, and has to be insulated. This is the "Handyman's Special."

The first house will net you something like $15,000 profit easily, the second house about $5000—if you are lucky.

For a true instance, the house that I called home for six years, the White House, at 91 Rumson Road in Rumson, New Jersey, was a mess when I first saw it. The house had been built in 1915, and looked as if the wallpaper had never been washed. The original curtains, handmade in Belgium, were hanging in tatters on the windows. The original rugs were disintegrating underfoot. In room after room, all 25 of them, the story was the same. The grounds were littered with boards and overpowered by weeds. I bought it for $80,000, from an estate after a number of people had looked it over and just turned away.

Now, I did spend some money on it, because 91 Rumson deserved it. I did some imaginative interior redesign: put in a modern kitchen in the solarium and hung first-class fancy wallpaper throughout. But the main effort was old-fashioned, sweaty clean-up.

At the end of six years, the house went up for sale. A buyer made a top bid of $395,000: profit, $128,000. That was a real recycle.

Shopping around for a Recycle

Instead of looking for a house you'd want to move into, you are looking for a house that you *wouldn't* want to move into. That dirty, uncomfortable mess may be the most profitable recycle around. I have moved into many such houses with a light heart, *knowing* here is money for the taking.

Recently I bought a house that had been on the market for quite some time with no takers. I had made a low bid, somewhat over $35,000, but the owner did not accept. (People are funny. If it's their home, they don't see how run-down it looks. They are comfortable in it and *they* like it. Therefore, they are puzzled when there are no takers.)

This particular owner had kept a dog, and the house smelled

terrible. There were dog hairs everywhere. Dirty rugs. Floors dark with ground-in grit. Walls with dents and holes. But it was a prime example of a recycler's opportunity: a house with simple needs that could be bought way below the potential market.

The owner finally accepted my bid three months later. I deodorized, disinfected, washed and spackled wallboard, repainted, put in new rugs, new curtains, and a new kitchen. I spent less than $15,000. I wiped my brow, put on clean clothes, and put an ad in the real estate section. Within two weeks, the house sold for $64,000. Profit, $14,000.

Such profitable houses are not for sale every day, but *they are out there*.

Middle-of-the-Ladder Recycles

Let's look at middle-of-the-ladder recycles for a moment: those numbered 5 through 8 on the ladder. These middle-of-the-ladder needs cost more to fill, but on the other hand, once the improvements are in, the house's value jumps more than a bottom-of-the-ladder recycle.

Many times, the main improvement needed is modernizing the kitchen. Replace the old-fashioned iron sink, add matched cabinets, new linoleum, and a dishwasher (don't try to sell a house without one). If you shop comparatively and look for sales on the big ticket items, you can do all this for less than $5000. It may take you three months of part-time work, if you do all the replumbing and rewiring yourself. So, for $5000 cash, you have increased the value of the house $10,000 to $15,000. That's quick profit.

The kitchen is a key to the market price of any house. The kitchen today reflects the status of the owners in the way the Victorian parlor did 100 years ago. A good-looking kitchen is a must.

Now, very briefly, let's consider top-of-the-ladder recycles. The cost of improvement is higher and the work is more complicated, but you get correspondingly bigger jumps in market value. A typical example is adding a new bathroom where none exists. The market value can jump easily three times your improvement cost. But *don't*, as your first recycle, take on a house with more than one, or—at most—two top-of-the-ladder needs.

Looking for a Recycle

The first place to start looking is at home. Does your own house have the combination of needs that will allow you to possibly double the price when recycled? Very likely not. (When you go looking for a house to recycle, you look for a house you *wouldn't* want to live in.) So you start looking at other houses.

You look for a house that lacks what other houses in the neighborhood *have*. You are also looking for a house that is being sold for less than the "ceiling" for that type of house in that neighborhood. There's a top price for, say, a two-bedroom, two-bath house in a given neighborhood, no matter how fancy the house is. You are looking for a house priced under the ceiling for some reason; you remove the reason and bring the house up to the ceiling.

One of my recycles was a two-story decrepit-looking building with a ruined kitchen floor (from storm tides washing through), that I bought for $4000. Shortly after I started work, a kid from the neighborhood came wandering by and said, "Why did you buy this junky old house? My mother says it's the worst house in the neighborhood." Bless his heart. He let me in on the secret.

In a few months, the recycling work I had done pushed the value of the house to $15,000. By the time I had finished renting it and had sold it, the profit was more than $42,000—on a total investment of $18,000! Precisely because it *was* the worst house in the neighborhood.

Later on, I found that the wonderfully built but neglected Victorian houses in my immediate area were just as profitable to recycle. Their beautiful wainscoting, carved ceilings, and curved bannisters, (common features in the early 1900s) were too expensive to put into a newly built house today. And for this very reason a Victorian makes a bigger jump in market value.

Up Neighborhoods and Down Neighborhoods

The recycler does not count on the automatic rise (appreciation) in the house's price to beat inflation, but welcomes it as additional profit. On the other hand, he avoids the neighborhood where the house values remain fixed or decline. You must make *sure* the neighborhood is on the upswing. Otherwise, your recycling profit could be jeopardized.

If you really want to be an "urban pioneer," make sure that you haven't gone too far beyond the "frontier." Polonius in *Hamlet* was a windbag but his "Be not the first by whom the new is tried" applies here.

House location is of utmost importance. Whole cities and towns are either *up* or *down*. Towns on the "up" cycle have decreased in the Northeast "Snow Belt" and increased in the Southwest "Sun Belt." But if you live in the Northeast, you still can find good "up" situations there, particularly in resort or vacation areas. And you can find good recycling in a town that is being discovered by artists and craftsmen, or wherever new modern, clean, high-technology-type industries are developing. This will send the up-curve sailing across the charts for decades.

Getting to Know the Place

The greatest profit comes to recyclers who have a solid grasp of the local scene. You need to learn *everything*.

I received a letter from a couple after my first book had been published. They wanted advice. They had a house under recycle in one town, and another a hundred miles off in another town, and were looking at another house even farther away. They weren't taking the time to look closely anywhere. This is dangerous. They could easily get into a "down" neighborhood, or into a "down" town. They were not doing their homework.

They had not talked to people in the real-estate business. Also, they obviously had not searched carefully enough to find that one house in fifty that would give them the maximum chance to make maximum profits. Sure, they might make 10 percent on the money they invest. But anyone can do that well in a money market fund—without all the work and bother.

Know your territory!

part II

Getting the Most Out of a Good Situation

4

The Weir Fifty Percent Rule: Sure-Fire Recycles

In this chapter we go into the crucial second step of recycling: finding houses that are "Sure-Fire" profit makers, and bidding low for them. The connecting link here is something called the *Weir Fifty Percent Rule*.

This rule states that whether you rent or sell, your estimated market value after recycling has to be 50 percent *more* than the cost of the house plus estimated "costs of recycling."

Let's take the simplest case: You buy a house for $50,000 and you put $15,000 (cost of recycling) into it. You should see a market price of at least 50 percent more than you spent. Since you spent $50,000 to buy the house, plus $15,000 for materials the total equals $65,000. And 50 percent more than that is $97,500.

So, right at the beginning, you should see a potential market value of $97,500 for that house. Otherwise you have too small a margin for error to take a chance on recycling it.

Now comes the use of the *Weir Fifty Percent Rule* in bidding. The owner will be asking a price. Can you bid what he is asking? Do the arithmetic in the example given backwards to reach the figure for your bid. In this instance, figure what the house will sell for when recycled (make three brokers swear it on a Bible). If it will bring $97,500 recycled and it will cost you $15,000 to recycle it, the highest you can bid is $50,000. This may be a "low bid" as far as the owner is concerned, but is just right as far as you are concerned. *The Weir Fifty Percent Rule gives you a good general guideline to ensure a good profit.*

How to Figure Your Bid Under the Rule

We just gave a single figure for the "cost of recycling" in our first example. Actually "cost of recycling" is made up of two parts: One is the *cost of all the recycling materials* (and outside labor); the second is called *carrying costs* which includes everything else, such as cost of interest, lawyer's fees, insurance, etc. for the duration.

Let's say five brokers have told you a house will sell for $75,000 when recycled. This is the figure you start with, then. Now you can quickly figure that you can spend no more than $50,000 total on that house. I call this the *Weir Limit*, the most you can pay out for the whole recycle (arrived at by applying the Weir Fifty Percent Rule—$75,000 is exactly 50 percent more than the *Weir Limit* of $50,000.)

OK, now you estimate that your cost of recycling materials will be $10,000 and your carrying costs will be $5,000. Now you have all the facts needed to figure your bid. You know you are spending $10,000 on materials, and $5,000 on carrying costs. That is a total of $15,000. So you subtract the $15,000 from the $50,000 (Weir Limit). You see that you have exactly $35,000 left to buy the house with. So, $35,000 is your bid.

The house may be advertised at $50,000, or more. It may be that your bid of $35,000 is so low that the seller won't consider it—at least not right away. But you have to get *used* to bidding low and losing many more houses than you buy. You may *look* at 50 and *bid* on 20 to *get* one great recycle.

The Three Ways of Making Money Recycling

When you recycle, your profit comes from one or more of three processes: 1. recycling a house and renting it, 2. recycling a house and selling it, and 3. recycling it and collecting a speculation profit. A great recycle will often combine all three ways of making money on a house.

First you recycle it and rent it. Then you sell it at a good profit because of improvements. And if you are lucky, you also get the benefit of the appreciation (rise in value of the house greater than inflation, improvements aside).

Take these one at a time.

Rentals: Not every recycle is suitable for a rental, only the ones you can rent to compete in the low-cost rental market. That means you probably have to buy a single-family house at no more than $50,000. This is a house you can recycle and rent for something less than $700 to $1000 a month. If you have to charge more than that (depending on location in the U.S.), you will be competing with luxury rentals, a class in which you cannot be competitive since luxury rentals can offer more amenities, usually.

Secondly, a renter who can pay more than $700 to $1000 a month can probably also *buy* a house as an alternative to renting. So the high-rental market is not one where the recycler competes well.

So far, so good. Now let's see how the Weir Fifty Percent Rule applies to rentals, to give you a Sure-Fire rental, or *Sure-Fire Type I* house.

Sure-Fire Type I: Rental

In figuring rentals, figure yearly costs. Here is a house that you buy for $40,000. This breaks up into a $15,000 down payment and $25,000 mortgage. It will cost $3000 to recycle. It will have $2000 in carrying costs the first year. So, you have a $5000 recycling cost. You convert all costs to yearly costs by converting all the amounts to loans and figuring the first year installment payments on the loans.

Payments on a twenty-year 15 percent mortgage loan of $25,000	$4000
Payments on a twenty-year 15 percent $15,000 down-payment loan	$2000
Payments on a seven-year $5000 home improvement loan	$1200
	$7200

In other words, the house is going to cost you $7200 "cash-out" the first year, nearly as much the second year, and somewhat less each succeeding year. You therefore have to see at least 50 percent more each year—at least $10,800 a year ($900 a month) coming in via rental to make this house a candidate for a rental recycle. Otherwise, your margin for error will be too small and you may lose money on your rental.

Here is an easy way to figure the Fifty Percent Rule in rentals: Figure them by the month. Every creditor will give you "monthly installment" figures for his loan; banks have it all marked on their little mortgage payment stubs. Let's say your monthly costs add up this way:

Mortgage payment	$300
Down-payment loan	200
Materials loan	50
Carrying charges loan	150
	$700

You need roughly $1000 rental income a month by the Weir Fifty Percent Rule. If you can do that, then you have a *Sure-Fire Type I* recycle, a sure-profit rental.

One way to get $1000 out of the house easily is to turn it into a duplex and charge each family $500 a month for a total of

$1000. But, if you can't see $1000 in rent coming in, then you don't rent it—just buy it, recycle, and sell it.

Sure-Fire Type II: Buy-Recycle-Sell

Let's say that you are buying the house for $60,000 and the cost of recycling is $20,000. Then you have an $80,000 total outlay. To successfully buy-recycle-sell, you should see a market price on the house of 50 percent more, or $120,000. In other words, once the house is improved, if the potential market price is $120,000 (or 50 percent more than you put into it), then you have a Sure-Fire Type II—a profitable buy-recycle-sell house.

Will you ever find a house for $60,000 that will sell, fixed-up, for $120,000? That sounds like a big jump in market value—and it is. You will usually have to look at a good many houses—say fifty—before you get that kind of deal. Always *wait* for it. That kind of deal will come along, eventually.

You need that kind of margin. A recycler is allowed exactly zero big mistakes. One big mistake and you are *out*. We are playing with big money here and you (as a small entrepreneur) can only play with big money if you play it *real* safe. So, ideally, you look for a house that is some *combination* of Type I and Type II and/or Type III Sure-Fire recycles.

Sure-Fire Type III: Speculation

Since we haven't talked about Sure-Fire III yet, let's do it. Sure-Fire Type III is the profitable speculation-recycle property. This is also the standard real estate investment, the so-called "investment property." Everybody is out looking for this rare kind of property. Even without improvement, it gains value *faster* than inflation and therefore produces a profit whether you recycle it or *not*. So, while you are always on the lookout for a Type III situation, you don't really *need* it, the way a speculator does. If you are lucky enough to get it, so much the better. If not, you *still* make a good profit from rental and/or buy-recycle-sell.

If you are really clever at searching, or if some real estate agent loves you very much, you might get hold of a property that increases in value by 15 or 20 percent per year—beating out inflation by a considerable amount. And *then* you add a successful speculation-recycle profit (Type III) to your buy-recycle-sell profit (Type II) and rental-recycle profit (Type I). Nice work if you can get it.

In general, particularly today, you cannot *count* on speculation profit. But you can *count* on your improvement-profit and/or rental-profit. Be wary of "negative" speculation profit: neighborhood values going down, rather than up (as discussed in the previous chapter). You cannot count on making speculation profit, but you can *prevent* "speculation loss."

The Art and Necessity of Low Bids

Successful recycling depends on successfully making *low* bids, some of which are *accepted*. Since very few houses are going to sell for a low bid, guess what? You will usually have to look a long time, just to get that one house that will really make you richer.

Sometimes I compromise and bid a *little* higher than called for by the Weir Fifty Percent Rule, but not often. On the average I discipline myself to the painstaking search, house after house.

People often say to me, "Boy were you lucky. You hit the rising price curve in the housing market just as it started to go up. I wish I had thought of that." The statement makes me smile as I remember the weary work of looking at thousands of houses to select a few so carefully. One definition of *genius* is "an infinite capacity for taking pains."

The Psychological Side of Low Bidding

The question arises when a house is up for sale at a low price: Do you make a quick "guess bid" before anyone else bids, or take your time and make a rough "cost of recycling estimate" and then make a more thought-out bid according to the Weir Fifty Percent Rule?

Let's say you look at a run-down house that has potential market value of $60,000 and it's up for sale at $35,000 (just above half the potential market price). You are always safe in making a "guess-bid" of half the potential market value ($30,000 in this case) as long as the house only has bottom or middle-of-the-ladder needs. By bidding fast, you may get it, bang! like that, at a bargain price.

But suppose the owner is asking $45,000 for the same house. That house is not going to be bought all that quickly—his asking price is too high. So you have time to make a rough recycling plan and make a more deliberate bid using the Fifty Percent Rule. Depending on the house, your "deliberate bid" can be considerably *more* than half the potential market value, thus giving you a better chance of getting the house and still making a profit.

Be diplomatic whenever you make a low bid. Say something to the owner like, "I realize that this bid is low, but it is all that I can afford to spend on the house. You will probably get a higher bid than mine, but for the record this is how much I can pay. Good luck." The owner will at least realize that you do want the house, so you will leave an avenue of communication open. He may then come back in a month or two and accept.

A home is part of the owner's ego. If he can't get the price he wants, he may well sell at a lesser price to someone he thinks *does* want it. And at that point, you have a bargain.

Another way of working is to bid through an agent. That way, if there are some negative feelings about the low bid, the owner won't be looking you right in the eye. The real estate agent's job is to soothe the owner in such a case.

In any case, every so often a low bid will get it. Once I bid $37,500 on a house for which the owner was asking $50,000 (at 11 Center St., in Eatontown, N.J.). The price I bid was based on the Weir Fifty Percent Rule. Three months later, the owner came back and accepted that bid. I was in business: profit $17,000.

The Discipline of Low Bidding

Let's say you read an ad for a house with two bedrooms and two baths, for $75,000. After investigating, you found that same-size houses with two baths and two bedrooms on that street are going for $120,000.

Very interesting. You get in touch with the agency listing it and ask, "Why is it priced so low?" The agent says it has been neglected; it is up for sale as part of an estate, but looks so bad there have been no takers so far. It begins to sound exciting.

A quick guess-bid would be half the potential market value or $60,000, but since the house is offered at considerably more than half the potential market value, it is not going to be snapped up. Therefore, you have time to figure cost, and apply the Weir Fifty Percent Rule. You figure that you can recycle the house for $15,000 in materials and carrying costs. Under the Weir Fifty Percent Rule, you can bid $65,000 for the house, which is more likely to be accepted than the quick bid of $60,000 would have been. But by no means go *above* $65,000 in such a case, particularly if this is your first recycle. The discipline of staying with the Weir Fifty Percent Rule (when you really *want* to bid more) pays off. Wait for that house where your low bid is accepted. This rule has worked fantastically well for me.

Review: The Nine Steps of Recycling

1. Finding a house with the right needs in the right neighborhood.
2. Spotting Sure-Fire combinations and bidding low.
3. Getting an advantageous mortgage and other financing.
4. Closing on the purchase legally and conclusively.
5. Making a detailed recycling plan to control costs.
6. Blazing a paper trail to ensure nonstop recycling.
7. Recycling the house systems (plumbing, heating, etc.).
8. Recycling the exterior, interior, and landscaping.
9. Using selling know-how to get a profitable seller.

5

Finding a Bank Mortgage for Your 1980s Inflation-Beater

Now we take up the first part of Step 3 of recycling: getting a bank mortgage loan. Bank mortgages are the mainstay of recycling (although there are other sources for mortgages, as we shall see).

A mortgage is a loan which is *secured* by the property (more on the meaning of "secured" later). Traditionally, it is paid back in small monthly installments over twenty to thirty years. A bank will usually loan you up to three-quarters of the current market value of the house on a mortgage. The other one-quarter you have to supply. This is the "down payment."

The first, and by far the most vital, reason why the bank mortgage is so important is that the mortgage's low installment payments protect the recycler's cash flow.

The recycler needs cash flow for many things. He may need it to pay installments on loans made to cover the down payment, for materials needed to recycle, or for carrying charges on the house. If he runs out of cash, he has to stop the recycle.

Should a recycler borrow all this money on short-term (personal) loans, he then has large installment payments to make, which cut into his cash flow. So a recycler protects his cash flow by getting as much of his financing from long-term low-installment mortgage loans (secured) as he can. A recycler has an advantage over the average house buyer when it comes to mortgages, as we explained earlier.

To recap: Let us say a recycler gets a low-interest rate of 10 percent on a loan of $30,000. He will have paid $3000 interest by the end of the recycle year. Now, if he gets a loan at a higher rate of 15 percent, then on a mortgage of $30,000 the recycler will pay $4500 for the year, or $1500 more. So it costs the recycler relatively little to borrow money at a "high" rate because he can usually sell the house within a year of buying it.

How to Learn about Mortgages

Banks are the most experienced and convenient institutions for giving you a mortgage loan. Bank loan officers have been through the mortgage transaction so many times they generally deal wisely with any given mortgage situation. The banks are thus the number one source for mortgages.

Your own situation is unique. The situation in your town and county is unique. The time is unique; what the banks did last month may have little bearing on what they do this month, and they may do something different next month. You have to find that out. Don't be hesitant to go to your own bank to ask questions. And then get another point of view from another bank.

As for myself, even though I have been dealing with mortgages for more than ten years on an almost weekly basis, I still quite often sit down with a bank officer to ask questions. I'm not worried about "looking dumb." Never was. Part of my success as a recycler came from always having the guts to ask.

If you don't currently use a bank, establish a savings account or a checking account in a nearby bank. Then get hold of one of the loan officers in the bank. Tell him you are interested in buying a house and that you want the basic information about mortgages. Make notes on the conversation.

Then borrow or buy a simple textbook on mortgages. You can get them at the library or any textbook store. Read up a bit, and go over your notes. Let some of the ideas sink in.

Then go back to the loan officer with a list of written questions and get the answers. What you are doing is slowly building up some understanding of mortgage finance, which is very important. In today's world, the mortgage situation is very fluid and complex, and much more complicated to deal with than it was even three or four years ago.

This procedure for finding out about mortgages is the kind of thing that your education should have trained you to do. Unfortunately, the educational system often convinces you that it is dumb to ask questions. Combining book knowledge with interviewing people engaged in local mortgage financing (lawyers specializing in real estate, bankers, brokers, and accountants) can work wonders for your perception of how to finance a recycle.

Everything, no matter how creative and artistic, uses one basic building material—money. Finding out about money gives you insight into what makes the world go 'round.

The Traditional Bank Mortgage

Banks make some money on mortgages, but not very much (say 2 percent on the average). The reason they don't make money is that banks have to first borrow all the money that they lend out. They borrow from Peter to lend to Paul. The rate at which banks can borrow is effectively controlled by the U.S. government. So if the government decrees that the interest paid by banks shall rise, the banks in turn have to raise the rate they *charge* those who borrow from them. Banks usually charge only a couple of percent more than they have to pay for the money. Thus, the mortgage loan is more of a bank *service* than a real money-making deal.

The banks use their mortgage loans to attract customers to other services. They can charge a relatively higher rate, such as personal loans. The banks also use mortgage loans to get customers to open savings accounts (another source of revenue for the bank).

Thus, a bank would *like* to give you a mortgage. Provided, of course, that the bank has mortgage money to give, and provided you *qualify* as a "good risk."

We will get into what makes a recycler a good risk in a minute. But first, let's look more closely at mortgage loans.

The mortgage loan is based on the fact that every house, even a poorly built one, needing all kinds of work, has a certain market value. A good "appraiser" who knows the market can assess the house's "appraised value."

In the usual mortgage transaction, the buyer sees a house that he wants and bids on the house, "contingent on getting a mortgage." Then he goes to a bank and asks what kind of mortgage he can get, and for how much. The bank sends out its appraiser, and the appraiser gives the house a value (what the appraiser thinks the market value really is). The bank loans up to three-quarters the appraised value to the prospective buyer.

The mortgage contract allows the buyer to pay back the mortgage principal and interest over a long period of time. But the mortgage contract also specifies that the bank has the right—if the buyer fails to pay the installments—to repossess the house and sell it to raise the remaining unpaid principal. The house itself "secures" the mortgage.

It is a safe deal for the bank. The house buyer (borrower) is going to move heaven and earth to pay the installments. Otherwise the buyer is out of his house. In that case, he loses the chance to make a profit reselling it, and loses his living quarters. Worst of all, he could lose his 25 percent down payment, if the forced sale doesn't cover the whole principal.

Thus, the relatively low rate that the bank charges on the mortgage loan is justified by the fact that the bank runs very little risk of losing money. Defaults on the part of the mortgage borrower are rare.

The Remortgage Gambit: Equity

If a recycler is buying his first house, he is depending on the bank to give him a loan on the appraised value of the house. But if the recycler already owns a house, he can get additional mortgage money by "remortgaging" the house he is living in.

With two mortgages, he may be able to get his entire recycle financed at the low payment rate afforded by mortgages, a situation which is ideal.

Here is how remortgaging works. The key word is "equity." Equity is simply a share of the house. At the beginning, with your first house the bank lends you three-quarters of the appraised value and then the bank's equity is three-quarters. Your equity is one-quarter. Then, as you pay off the installments, *your* equity increases. If you buy a house for $20,000 down with a $60,000 mortgage and you pay off $15,000 of the mortgage principal (along with paying off the interest), your equity now equals $35,000 (up from $20,000—the down payment). The bank's equity now equals $45,000 (down from $60,000, the original mortgage). The longer you hold the mortgage and pay installments, the greater your equity and the less the bank's.

And here is the nice thing: Your equity can increase not only as a result of paying installments, but as a result of the value of the house increasing on the market (appreciation). If you buy a house at $80,000 and find that after two years—when you have paid off $5,000 of the principal—the house will now sell for $95,000, your equity has increased not only by the $5000 you paid off but by the $15,000 the house went up in value. Thus, if your down payment was $20,000, your equity has gone up $5000 through installments plus $15,000 through appreciation (rise in value). Your equity has doubled to $40,000! Now by "remortgaging," you can "get part of that equity out."

Let's say you go to the bank and ask to remortgage your house. The bank gives you a new $70,000 mortgage (three-quarters of appraised value of $95,000). You pay off the old mortgage; that leaves you with a spare sum of $15,000 to use on the new recycle. Thus, you still own your house, and you have $15,000 cash to put against the recycle of another house. This is what "refinancing" can do for you.

Can You Remortgage a Converted Barn?

Let's look at the notion of *appraised value*. You go in to see a bank loan officer and say: "Well, sir, I have this marvelous old barn that I moved into. Got it cheap: $10,000 cash. Now I want to recycle it: put in heat, running water, bathrooms, and a new roof, plus reshingle it. Can you give me a $10,000 mortgage to do that?"

Chances are ten out of ten the bank says no. Why? Isn't a barn a perfectly good home? Won't it be worth much more than $10,000 when you finish recycling it?

Ah, yes. But mortgages are made on the house's appraised value right now. Right now the barn is uninhabitable and has almost no appraised value, even if you did pay $10,000 for it.

Any loan made on the *future* value is a "risk capital" loan. The interest rate for risk capital is much higher—the deal may include a share of the profits.

A mortgage loan is not a risk capital loan. If you think it is, you only mistake the nature of mortgages and miss the reason for the low rates.

Recyclers Deal with Low Appraisals

Since a recycled house is often in poor shape when it is bought, it will be appraised at a rather low value compared to its potential future market value. So the recycler may not get much of a mortgage on the house he wants to recycle. Thus, a house may be worth $120,000 recycled but be in such poor shape as to only be appraised at $40,000. The bank will only give the recycler a $30,000 mortgage. You have to raise the rest of the money elsewhere (see the next chapter).

What Makes You a Good Risk?

Now, we've learned about appraised value; let's go on to the subject of how to qualify for a mortgage, or a remortgage.

In a remortgage, you have to have equity in a house you own to secure the loan. Or, if it's a new mortgage, the house you are about to buy has to have appraised value to secure the loan. (That is pretty obvious.) Then you have to be able to come up with a down payment in some fashion—either short-term borrowing or a remortgage, or from cash on hand.

But now we come to the less obvious things. There are always more people who want to borrow on mortgage terms than there is mortgage money available from banks. Thus, the bank looks for *qualifications*. The most qualified people get a "Yes." And the others get a "No." To put it in other terms, a bank loans money to the better risks first.

How do you get to be a good risk? There are a number of factors.

1. *Commitment*. The banker (in looking for commitment) looks at whether or not you are going to live in the house, either during or after the recycle. The banker senses commitment if you let him know you want very much to live in the new house.

2. *General preparation*. Knowing where to get the skills (assuming you can't demonstrate you have them yourself) to do the necessary work. If you have a contractor's list of materials needed and a commitment from a local plumber to do the plumbing work and an agreement with a local contractor to do the heavy construction work, then you will begin to be convincing. By contrast, nothing will turn a banker off more than the feeling that you are not prepared, that you may tear the house apart and then quit in frustration because you are not sure how to finish the work. Saying to a banker, "There's this house, see, and I want to learn to recycle houses, so I am just going to go in there and start pulling down walls," is *not* being convincing.

3. *Financial plan*. List how you are going to raise all the sums (besides the mortgage that you are applying for). The banker

wants to know that you can "hack it" financially and won't run out of money halfway through. The banker must be sure that you are able to complete the recycle, and that you won't leave him with a half-finished house with very little present market value. In such a case the bank would have to repossess the house, hire a contractor to finish the work, then sell it. The last thing a bank wants to get into is the real estate business.

4. *Recycle plan.* This is a sketch in words (and maybe drawings) of what you are going to do to change the house, how you plan to proceed, the amount and kind of materials needed, where you plan to get the materials, and how much they will cost.

Although I often work from inspiration and change my mind during the course of a recycle, I always have a rough recycling plan to start with.

Other Convincing Factors

Four more factors are important:

5. *Previous use of the bank.* If you have had a savings or checking account at the bank in question, and particularly if you have borrowed and repaid a previous loan, you stand a better chance than if you have never had previous bank dealings. A bank may not talk to you seriously unless you have had some sort of previous dealings with it. I keep accounts in a dozen different New Jersey banks for just that reason.

6. *Income other than recycling.* A part-time recycler will undoubtedly hold down a regular job of some kind and a bank likes that. A steady, reliable income that does not depend on the success of a recycle will go far toward making the bank give you a "Yes."

(A bank looks over your whole cash position. It wants to know what other installment loans you have. Banks won't loan money to anyone paying out more than a quarter of his monthly income in installments.)

7. *Assets other than the recycle.* Many people have assets that they are not aware of: an expensive car, a diamond ring that

could be sold for several thousand, stocks or bonds—anything that you can convert to cash in a hurry if you need it.

8. *Reliability.* You have to appear to be reliable and sound. Be well dressed, well groomed, sincere in manner, and energetic in presenting your qualifications—all in moderation. The banker wants to know that you are a reliable person who will buckle down and work your way out of a tight spot, if need be.

If you score well in: (1) Commitment, (2) Preparation, (3) Financial plan, (4) Recycle plan, (5) Previous use, (6) Income, (7) Assets, (8) Reliability, you qualify for the mortgage.

There Is More than One Bank

The next question is whether or not the bank has the mortgage money to loan for your particular location. If a bank turns you down, it is not the end of the world. It may be that the bank has run over its mortgage quota for the month, and while it says "No" this month, it will say "Yes" the next.

Another nearby bank may be more interested in lending mortgages in your particular location. Your real estate agent will know that. His business depends not only on selling you a house but on helping you find the mortgage money to pay for it.

And an experienced real estate lawyer will help a great deal; he knows the bankers in the field. So, it is not only a question of qualifying, but of qualifying at the right bank at the right time. Keep on applying.

Creative Bank Mortgage Approaches

The most pressing need the bank has today, other than assuring itself that you are a good risk, is to protect itself against loaning money at the present rate when next month it could have loaned the same money at a higher rate. As a result, most banks today won't give traditional mortgages. The banks want some way of adjusting for a rising interest rate.

One approach is a "balloon" mortgage. A balloon is a point at which the entire remaining mortgage principal is due: usually three or four years down the line. At that point, you renegotiate the interest rate on the remaining principal. This gives the bank a chance to raise it to current levels. This is called "rolling the loan over."

Today all banks more readily give a variable-interest-rate mortgage than a fixed-rate mortgage. They need to know the interest they get on the mortgage can be matched up with the fluctuations of the commercial interest rate.

Even so, before they are willing to give a mortgage, some banks will ask for a "partnership mortgage" in which they get a part of any resale profit. Since the recycler knows how to maximize this profit, this means giving the bank a good healthy chunk of money. The partnership mortgage is a last resort only. You can still make a profit, but your aim is to keep as much of the profit as possible, not give it away.

A recycler takes the time to find out about mortgages, in order to get the proper type of financing best fitted to his particular needs.

6

Completing the Financing and Closing the Recycle Deal

Thus far we have considered only the traditional bank mortgage as a source for financing the recycle. This is the "first mortgage," which gives the bank the "first right" to repossess the house and sell it to pay the remainder of the mortgage in case of default. But there is another kind of bank mortgage worth considering: the "second mortgage" on your own house.

Second Mortgage Financing

The second mortgage is "secured" by the lender's right to any money left over from the sale of the house after the holder of the first mortgage has been paid off—up to the amount of the second mortgage loan. Why would there be any money left over? Well, if the house, which was mortgaged for $50,000 (in addition to a $25,000 down payment), has appreciated and is now worth $150,000, then there is plenty of money left over after the first mortgage is paid off by a forced sale. The equity has increased.

Thus, a second mortgage is an alternative way besides remortgaging to convert part of your equity to cash so you can use it for further recycling.

In second mortgage financing you take out a second mortgage on your present house. A bank may give you a second mortgage equal to as much as three-quarters of the amount of your equity.

Let's take an example. An owner has made a down payment of $10,000 and has paid off $20,000 of the principal on a $40,000 mortgage, thus building up his equity to $30,000. A bank will lend him $22,500, three-quarters of his equity, on a second mortgage.

The recycler owning a house can take out a second mortgage without losing the low interest rate he is paying on the first mortgage. (Interest rates have climbed steadily through the last two decades.) Of course, he still can take out, in addition, a first mortgage on the house he recycles. Between the second mortgage on his own house and the first mortgage on the recycled house, he often can finance a recycle quite handily.

The Private Mortgage Sources

There is no reason why a *bank* has to be the mortgage lender. Your sister, parent, or good friend can make a mortgage loan contract with you, privately. Some "private lenders" make their living by giving first or second mortgage loans.

The most frequent kind of private loan is the "owner mortgage" or "take-back mortgage." The common expression, in such a case, is that "the owner is willing to take some paper back," that is, make a loan to help the buyer purchase the house.

Why would an owner want to do that?

If the owner wants to sell the house quickly, and the buyers can't find a willing bank, the owner may be willing to give a mortgage.

Other sources for first and second mortgages are credit unions, labor unions, employee associations, and personal finance organizations. Any sound, experienced accountant or

Short-Term Financing Sources

Everything else (except mortgages) usually comes under the heading of "short-term financing." This means that the principal and interest of the loan is all due within the year (sometimes longer, but usually for no more than five years).

It is theoretically possible to finance a whole recycle with short-term loans. On one of my projects, the whole financing was done in recurring ninety-day loans. In this kind of loan, you pay the interest in advance (at the beginning of the ninety days), and then at the end of the ninety days you renegotiate and make a new loan for another ninety days ("roll the loan over"), and so on until the project is finished. At each renewal, the interest rate is renegotiated. On my particular project, no mortgage loans were available at the time.

Short-term loans are not advantageous to the recycle. They involve higher interest rates than mortgage loans, and the interest is often due ahead of time. The short-term loan interest rate can sometimes be brought down if the loan is "secured" by some personal property that is immediately convertible to cash, such as precious stones, an expensive car, or stocks and bonds.

The kinds of short-term financing that you can get will vary from bank to bank and town to town. Following is a listing of some of the types, to give you an idea.

Construction loan. This is a loan that is given in installments by a bank on a schedule of items you complete as your construction proceeds. The last of the construction loan can be paid off by obtaining a regular mortgage after the construction is finished and the house is ready for occupancy. In the case where a recycle needs extensive exterior rebuilding, a bank will usually not give much of a *mortgage* loan on it but *will* give a construction loan on your personal credit rating.

Passbook loan. This loan is secured by the money in your

savings account. The money stays in the account and draws interest while you pay a slightly higher rate on your loan than you get on your savings.

Credit cards. You can borrow money on some credit cards or use them to pay for materials used in recycling.

Life insurance loan. You can borrow against the cash value of your life insurance policy from the life insurance company.

Home improvement loan. This is a five- to seven-year loan given specifically for home improvement, secured by equity in the house.

Contractor's loan. This is like a construction loan. The contractor doing work for you will defer payment until you can mortgage the house or otherwise raise the cash.

Supplier's loan. A building supply house may let you run up a bill at 18 percent (or more) interest until you sell the house and pay off the bills.

Unusual Money Sources

A sometimes overlooked source of money is the "right to subdivide." If you have property that has subdivision rights, the property can be split so that a part of the land or a second house on the property can be sold off while you retain ownership to the rest. In this situation, you sell *part* to get financing for recycling the *rest.*

Several of my projects during the first ten years were financed partly by sales of a subdivided lot. (The previous owners had the right to subdivide but had never exercised the right.)

Then there is the FFL, "friends and family loan." This is a short-term loan from close relatives and acquaintances. My first recycle, at 18 Beach, was in part financed by a family loan of $2000. Small though the loan was, it gave just the boost needed to get the recycle going. (If you have a willing family, though, don't tap that source until you really need it; families are emergency equipment, not everyday sources.)

Sometimes there are "money men" in a community, men who lend money on unsecured loans, provided they have faith in the recyler. This kind of loan really comes under the heading of risk capital. The loan is made against probable future equity rather than on present equity. Money men will exact a good, stiff interest rate, and perhaps a slice of the profit. (If this is the only deal that you can make, then you have to keep your costs very low to make a profit from your recycle.)

Government Loan Sources

Governments, particularly the federal level, have (1) direct loan programs or (2) help for financial institutions to encourage home building. (It is an aim of government to encourage a stable, home-owning citizenry.) The main drawback here is paperwork and the consequent delays involved.

Federal Housing Authority. "Title I" backs bank loans at somewhat lower than market interest rates. Get the details from knowledgeable real estate agents or the nearest federal agency. Or call Washington, DC, directly and ask for the FHA phone number through the information operator.

The Veterans Administration. VA loans are available to veterans who buy houses or improve them.

Community Development The Department of Housing and Urban Development (HUD) has been giving up to $27,000 (repayable over twenty years) in urban areas that need revitalizing.

There's nothing lost in asking. If you don't ask what government loans are available now, you will never get one. You might find yourself eligible.

Figuring Your Bid under The Weir Rule

Let's say a house will sell for $150,000 when recycled. Since the formula is: Probable Selling Price = Weir Limit + 50 percent more, the probable selling price is $150,000 and the Weir Limit on this house is $100,000. Therefore, you know that you are going to plan to borrow (finance) $100,000, or come up with the cash in case your bid is accepted.

Knowing what we know now, we can sketch out a probable financial plan and, from that, figure a proper bid.

Materials and labor	$10,000
Carrying costs	20,000
Weir Rule Bid	70,000
(*Weir Limit*)	$100,000

So, the biggest item in carrying costs—the interest for a year—is calculated. Let's say you figure another $3000 for legal fees, taxes, and insurance for the year. Then your total carrying charges equal $17,000 plus $3000, or $20,000. The formula is: materials and labor + carrying cost + Weir Rule Bid = Weir Limit.

Your materials and labor cost, let's say, $10,000. You now have all the figures you need to calculate your bid.

Source of financing	*Principal*	*Interest*
Bank mortgage on the house to be recycled	$ 60,000	$ 9,000 (at 15%)
Second mortgage (own home)	30,000	6,000 (at 20%)
Credit card charges	5,000	1,000 (at 20%)
Home improvement loan	5,000	1,000 (at 20%)
(Weir Limit)	$100,000	$17,000 (year's interest)

Now you may not get the house for that bid, but maybe there are not that many people who want to put $30,000 into the house to fix it up. So, the owner might come around eventually if it is your bid or nobody's.

If he accepts, you are in business at the right price. You can make $50,000 easy if your estimates are accurate. Even if they are off by as much as 20 percent, you can still make $40,000 for the year's work. Or, say you get held up and had to spend two years instead of one doing the recycle; you'd still make $30,000. The Weir Fifty Percent Rule protects you against the unfortunate unforseen possibilities.

Let's suppose that you do *not* own a house when you start the recycle. How do you substitute for the money that was raised (in the example given) by the recycler's second mortgage on his own house? Well, you can ask the seller to give you a $30,000 second mortgage with a two-year balloon. Before the balloon matures, you will have sold the house and paid off the mortgages.

That ends Step 3, financing the recycle. Now we move to Step 4, which is "Closing the purchase legally and conclusively," the legal aspect of the sale.

Getting the Lawyer into It

Your lawyer ought to be experienced in real estate. There are plenty of good lawyers who know nothing about real estate (a very special part of the law). Your lawyer should know not only real estate, but the local political and social scene. He may see a deal is not healthy simply because of dubious people on the other side. Or he may know of negative conditions affecting the site: a sewer being laid with consequent large assessment, etc.

Wait until the lawyer says it's OK to give the "earnest money." Earnest money is customary in some locales. It simply means that you hand over a token sum (usually $100 to $500) to show you have some cash you can put your hands on. You get a receipt back. And once you actually sign, the lawyer can guide you through the step-by-step procedure of closing a deal quickly and profitably.

The Steps in Closing on the House

Real estate procedure is designed to keep useless negotiations to a minimum. Each party is gradually drawn into greater and greater commitment so that, while there is always opportunity to back out, the chance the deal will fall through lessens rapidly as the dealings proceed.

The next step toward a closing, after the verbal acceptance (and possibly earnest money), is the *contract of sale*. The contract of sale is handed around (don't mail them) and signed by everybody after preliminary negotiation between your lawyer and the owner's lawyer.

Contract of sale usually specifies (on the recycler's behalf) that the purchase is "contingent on a mortgage." No mortgage for you, no deal for him. And no penalty for you.

On the signing of the contract of sale you pay 10 percent of the purchase price, refundable if the mortgage falls through. The 10 percent shows that you are solvent. And when you get a mortgage, you are obliged to go ahead with the deal, or be liable to forfeit the 10 percent.

The contract of sale sets a time limit. The two parties agree to complete the requirements of the contract, each on his part, by a certain date (closing day) or the deal can legally be called off.

On that day the lawyers, the sellers, you the buyer, and the mortgaging bank (or other lender), will meet face to face to exchange money and documents in the proper order. (This is the *closing* itself.)

The contract of sale can contain stipulations regarding the furniture: what fixtures are to remain, what inspections the house must pass, what documents have to be obtained. In most cases, you can get a termite inspection. And if the plumbing looks poor, you can ask for an inspection by a plumber and get his opinion on the owner's assertion that the plumbing is fully working.

One clause you can consider putting in the contract of sale is a "time is of the essence." This means that the seller has to adhere to the closing date or pay any damages you suffer as a result of delay (such as postponing being able to rent the recycled house). A seller is usually not eager to have this clause put in because it makes him liable for delays he cannot control. But if you feel that the delay in the closing will cost you, you may want to insist on the clause. (As a matter of practical negotiating, I have never insisted on this clause, but there may come a time when I will do so.)

So much for the contract of sale. The next document to consider is the deed.

The Real Estate Deed

A deed is the formal insignia of ownership, the piece of paper that says you own the house. The deed not only says you are the owner, but it has a very detailed description of what you own.

Let's say the man who offers to sell you a house on Water Street in Tumbletown really believes that those elm trees he shows you along the property line are really on his land. (In fact, the elms are not.) This is where "the survey" comes in. You, the buyer, pay a surveyor to see that the boundaries described in the deed coincide with reality. (A bank usually requires a survey as part of the closing.)

The previous owner may not have had to have his property surveyed. So he may think he knows what the boundaries are, but he may be wrong. If the deed says that the land is half an acre, but the survey shows it to be only a third, then you can get the seller to come down in price, or withdraw entirely, if you wish.

The deed also lists the restrictions on your freedom of action: You may be in a development where all the owners have to sign an agreement on such things as size of the mailbox and whether or not you can add a front porch.

The deed also lists any "easements" on your land. An easement is a right of some outsider to trespass: to lay a phone line or electric cable across the land, or simply walk or drive along a certain part of it (a right of way). There may even be a "public right of way" because the public always walked along a certain path through your land.

Sometimes the present owner's deed may not describe all the easements, simply because they have never come to anyone's attention over the years. It is worth "walking the line," (touring the boundaries of the property) to see if there is a beaten dirt path across one corner of it indicating a "public right of way."

Title Search and Title Insurance

A title search ensures the legality of your title. You can have the title searched by your lawyer or a title insurance company (more expensive but more thorough). A title insurance company not only searches the title (makes sure that your deed is preceded by a legal series of previous deeds), but will also reimburse you for any loss incurred should the title be later claimed defective (clouded) in any way.

Suppose a relative of a previous owner shows up with what looks like a legal deed to the property—even though his deed has never been put into the local records. Then you may have a problem. Title insurance at least guarantees it won't be a money problem. They will go to court for you, as well as reimburse any drop in value of the land.

What if you find out that the phone company has the right to put poles and a cable across your land, but it wasn't mentioned in the deed? Then you have some money coming from the title insurance company, since the propery is now worth less than it seemed. The title insurance company can collect from the previous owner.

The Closing Itself

You can skip the closing and have your lawyer represent you, but it is possible that something might tangle in the final hour and you will need to be there to make decisions.

Oftentimes, since you have made a low bid, the seller will have been told by his friends that he sold out too cheaply. He may come in to the closing feeling resentful, looking for ways to back out, or at least to get more out of you. With a few deft and diplomatic moves, you may persuade the reluctant seller that you indeed want the property enough to hold him to his agreement, even if it makes him unhappy.

One thing you want to do just before the closing is go out and give the property a final inspection. Once a friend of mine bought a house *with* furniture, and she went out to inspect the house just before the closing and found that the owner had given all the furniture away. So she was due, and got, a rebate at the closing.

Another of my friends failed to go out to have a look. When the closing was over, he found that the previous owner had removed the drape pulls from the walls, the stove and refrigerator from the kitchen, and himself from the state to Florida.

Completing the Financing and Closing the Recycle Deal 55

You don't have to postpone the closing in cases where a problem like this comes up. The seller merely puts a sum of money up to be held by a third party "in escrow" to assure there is money to remedy the defect or pay for missing equipment.

(Once in an advertisement I had specified an "avocado green washer-drier." When the buyer made an inspection he found that the machines were plain white. The buyer refused to go through with the sale until I had put enough money into escrow to assure that he got the right color washer-drier.)

The closing can be a delicate thing. Everybody is nervous. At the conclusion of the closing, the new deed is handed over to you with your name on it. You have at that moment lessened control over your life by such outside forces as your boss, the Internal Revenue, and the landlord. You have begun to take your financial destiny into your own hands.

part III

Clearing the Way for Recycling the Profitable House

7

Making a Recycle Plan That Pays Off in the 1980s

This chapter focuses on Step 5 of recycling: making two recycle plans to control costs. Your first recycle plan is a "rough plan," a sketchy concept jotted down with rough estimates of recycle costs. This enables you to calculate your bid.

If your bid is accepted, you make a second, more detailed recycle plan. It is an item-by-item list of materials and labor costs. It serves two purposes: It helps you to refine your thinking and spell out your costs. The second recycle will help you convince a bank to give a mortgage.

The Rough Estimate: Purpose

If the rough estimate is low, you can bid higher and your chances of getting the house are better.

Let us say a house will sell for $120,000 when it is recycled.

The rough estimate for materials is, as you calculate it, $15,000. This means that your financial plan could look like this:

Market price when recycled	$120,000
Bid for house	55,000
Costs of materials (rough estimate)	15,000
Cost of interest, carrying costs	10,000
(Weir Limit)	$80,000

But suppose your materials costs are $20,000, instead of $15,000. Then your bid has to be $5000 less, or $50,000. (You have added $5000 to costs, so you have to take $5000 off the bid.) Again, suppose that your cost of recycling materials adds up to only $5000. Then, you can bid $65,000, or $10,000 more.

Making the Detailed Recycle Plan

To make a detailed plan, you refer to your rough recycle plan. Every change or renovation required by the plan calls for buying a certain amount of materials, even if it's just a can of cleanser, washrags, and a gallon of off-white paint. (Those items are sometimes all you need to renovate a room.) Write down on a pad what materials are needed for every change and renovation envisioned.

Take, for example, a single twelve-by-fifteen-foot room: You plan to paint the ceiling, wallpaper the walls and carpet the floor.

Ceiling paint	$ 50
Spackle	15
Paint for walls	85
Wallpaper	150
Carpet	250
	$550

Six rooms in the house (at this average cost) would come to

$3300. Now add to that (for a typical recycle) $5000 for a kitchen renovation and $2000 apiece for renovating two bathrooms, and you are up to $12,300 for the cost of materials.

(You could cut costs by just painting the walls rather than wallpapering—if this meets the neighborhood standard. And you could partially, instead of fully, renovate the kitchen if it's in pretty good shape now. And so on.) The real question is whether or not you can keep the cost of materials low enough to make the bid attractive to the owner.

I have often had friends tell me that I should recycle such and such a house because it is "a wreck." That is *not* the kind of house I am looking for, at all. I can tell just from hearing about it that a recycle of this half-ruined house would fail. I leave half-ruined houses to people whose hobby is fixing up half-ruined-houses-which-cost-a-fortune-to-fix. What I look for is a house where the recycle cost is low and thus in line with making a sizable, inflation-beating profit.

Raise It Ten Percent

Once you have your detailed estimate, raise it 10 percent. There is no way you can allow for every cost; there are always some surprises. So by adding (arbitrarily) 10 percent, you get control over those costs that you cannot foresee. You *must* not run out of cash. When you run out of cash, you run out of gas. Your recycle then has to wait on more cash. The longer it takes to recycle, the more you pay in interest. "The meter is running," as we say, and you can fall into the "running-out-of-gas trap."

Another trap is the "shoestring trap." You underestimate costs, and try to make it come out by cutting corners in the recycle to the point that the recycle isn't up to the neighborhood standard. Then it takes longer to sell the house at a decent profit. Your interest charges accumulate. A dilemma to avoid.

Using Good Materials

We will go into interior design in a later chapter, but let's now sketch in a few broad ideas relevant to making a recycle plan. The worst thing you can do in a recycle is use materials that are dull and old-fashioned. Create a bright look. The materials will cost a bit more, but every penny spent here is worth it. There are plenty of wallpapers, ceiling tiles, and floor carpeting (just to take a few items) that are cheerful and wear well. Your recycle plan ought to envision using tough, easily cleaned, attractive building and design materials.

For instance, I discovered "texture paint." You can use it on any rough wall. It fills out the small cracks and, at the same time, gives the wall a pleasing texture. A marvelous material.

Where do you get the information? (At least that is the right question.) Besides the literature (home builders' magazines, catalogs), another good source is people who work in building-/design/decorating. There are bound to be some around that you can talk to. And an architect may know useful people in town. Again, you have to do your own research.

Your local hardware store is one place to start. If they do any business with designers, etc., they will be glad to tell you whom they find easy to work with. The hardware store might also be able to tell you what materials are a good buy locally. What is inexpensive in Atlanta may not be in Pittsburgh.

When you are estimating the cost of installing or modernizing major house systems such as plumbing, heating, and electricity (which are dealt with later in the book), your most reliable source of information is the professional. You can bring one in to estimate the cost and then decide whether to do it or let him do it.

Better still, get estimates from two pros. Ask around at your hardware or building supply store and find out which plumbers, electricians, etc. have a good reputation for solid work and reasonable fees.

What Changes to Make

We go into house design in detail in a later chapter, but let's sketch out a few ideas here relative to making an estimate.

What changes do you make? In the ideal recycle, you walk in, clean up, touch up, brighten up, make a few simple changes, and thereby make the house salable. Of course, it is hardly ever that simple. If it were, you'd never need to make a recycle plan.

In the usual case, *some* interior or exterior redesign is needed. You change either the room layout inside, or the *look* of the house outside, by adding exterior elements or getting rid of some.

Let's assume you are going to make exterior changes. Then you want a formal, clean sketch—not only for the bank as a convincer, but for the sake of your own clear thinking. The whole design approach is to stay within the discipline of "less is more." The less you spend to raise the value a given amount, the *more* you profit.

For instance, if you have a house that "gets by" on its exterior appearance but does need good plumbing, then you do the plumbing but not the exterior (much as you would like to). If redoing the exterior is *not* going to raise the value all that much, then you simply don't do it. That's discipline.

Exterior Versus Interior Changes

Changes dictated by a recycle plan can be grouped into exterior, interior-structural, interior-nonstructural.

The least costly plan is changes only in the interior-nonstructural parts of the house. And these are the changes that add most to the house in terms of value-raising per dollar put in. So start looking for houses that do *not* need much exterior change; all exterior changes are expensive. (Exterior materials are expensive because they have to be rugged and weatherproof.)

If you see a house with a downright ugly weatherbeaten look, avoid it, unless ugly-and-weatherbeaten happens to be chic (as at the seashore in certain locales). A house that is frazzled-looking and has to have exterior repair or be reshingled is going to cost a lot to recycle. Given two houses, one needing interior and the other exterior changes, take the interior-needy house.

Extensive Exterior Changes

Sometimes there *is* a case for *extensive* exterior changes. For instance, on one recycle, I joined two small houses that were rather strange looking, and built a single roof over both. Instead of two little structures, the building became a single dwelling much improved in look. That one exterior change, although extensive, doubled the value of the house.

There are other kinds of value-raising extensive exterior changes that you can make. For instance, if you have a house with a fantastic view (as in overlooking a beach), you can "open toward the view" by adding picture windows and sliding glass doors on that side. I once went so far as to put a living room and kitchen on the second floor of a beach house to take advantage of an extraordinary view. In other words, just as in spotting "use needs" (Chapter 3), you can also spot *design needs* that pay off.

Gauging the Exterior Changes

Perhaps *none* of the houses in the neighborhood have clearstories or skylights, but you see that your house is dull and will stand out by having them. This is a good case for exterior change. So you put in a few skylights to make the house competitive. Now you will have curb appeal and attract buyers.

(If the house is a *great* house anyway and doesn't need anything special going for it, then you don't need clearstories and skylights. Gauging this sort of thing is very important in recycling.)

At the 16 Locust recycle, the simple addition of a four-by-four skylight in the master bedroom made a big difference in the attractiveness of the main bedroom, and gave the house a special appeal. It raised the value of the house a couple of thousand. The skylight cost $150.

Making Selling Easy

What you really want, as far as exterior changes are concerned, is a house that beats out the houses around it—visibly. But again, not by too great a margin. You can't "outbuild" the neighborhood. There is a limit beyond which you cannot persuade people to pay for the privilege of being the best house around. Putting a swimming pool in a middle-class, half-acre-lot kind of residential zone might be too much—unless it's Los Angeles.

On the other hand, it is even less productive to come onto the market with a house substandard for the neighborhood. The house will be hard to sell. The "meter is running" and you will be spending extra weeks showing it or discussing it with real estate agents—on and on—time that could have been much better spent in other ways. Having a house that does not sell is wearing psychologically, particularly if you are advertising it and showing it yourself.

Interior Planning Ideas

Let's say that a house you have just found is a perfect recycle; you need to make a few relatively minor changes. The small rooms can be enlarged by knocking down a few walls, and you can eliminate the hallway to make more room. So now, you are ready to make a detailed interior plan.

The first thing that I do when I want to make an interior plan is—don't make the plan. First, I clean out the house. By the time I am finished, my head has, on a subconscious level, come up with some ideas that I would never have had just trying to think about the house in the abstract. The trick is to get the *feel* of the house. Nothing beats cleaning as a way of doing that.

Be selective about what you keep. Never throw old moldings away; keep them until the house is done. Look at everything with a creative eye. Will two broken chairs make one good one? Perhaps the bottom part of the hutch would be usable if I removed the water-damaged top. If a door is missing to an armoire, take the other one off and end up with a great bookcase.

After you have cleaned, make an overall plan for each floor. Where do you want to take out walls, add walls, and how do you envision the furniture placement? A clean, if informal, sketch will show you whether or not your brainstorm is going to work.

Open Up the House

Open up the house as much as you can, making larger spaces out of smaller ones, getting rid of dead ends, stairwells, halls, and unnecessary closets. If the kitchen is small, break through the wall into the living room and put in a counter with bar stools. (An exhaust fan will keep kitchen smells from going through the house.)

Occasionally you get the other problem: You have a barnlike house that needs to be divided up. In that case, there is a good rationale for calling in an architect because it is much easier to redesign a house already in use than to set up a whole integrated pattern of use where none existed before. Architects are good at this. They do it all the time.

A house can always use another room; a top trick of my interior design is to come up with a new room out of space that was wasted before. You can sometimes find a solidly built porch to enclose. You can combine a back closet with a back porch and get a wonderful mudroom for hanging outdoor clothes and boots. You can convert attics into spare bedrooms, and storage lofts (with the help of a dormer) into a secluded study or sewing room.

The Structural Wall

If it were not there, the ceiling would fall down. This defines a structural or load-bearing interior wall. Nine out of ten interior

Above: Mary Weir's son Chris in front of recycled 91 Rumson Road.
Above right: Mary restoring a piece of decorative art. *Photo by Jeff Martin.*
Below: 91 Rumson Road fireplace room recycled. *Photo by Jeff Martin.*

Left: Mary and friend working at 91 Rumson Road. *Photo by Jeff Martin.*

Below left and center: 29 Monmouth Road, before and after being recycled.

Below: 27 Monmouth Road, before and after being recycled.

Above: Peninsula House, after being recycled. *Photo by Jeff Martin.*

Right: Mary working on Peninsula House Restaurant roof: Peninsula House Hotel in background. *Photo by Jeff Martin.*

Below: Mary Weir spackling sheet rock on the Peninsula House Restaurant ceiling. *Photo by Jeff Martin.*

Below bottom: Peninsula House, during restoration. *Photo by Jeff Martin.*

Near above: The lobby at Peninsula House, before. *Photo by Jeff Martin.*

Far above: The country hearth at Peninsula House. *Photo by Jeff Martin.*

Right: The lobby at Peninsula House, after being recycled. *Photo by Jeff Martin.*

Below: The upstairs dining room at Peninsula House. *Photo by Jeff Martin.*

Right: 11 Center, before and after being recycled.

Right and below: Linden's kitchen, during restoration and after being recycled.

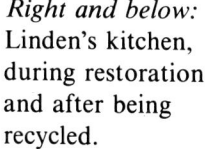

walls do not bear any load from the upper floors. Then there is that tenth one which does, and you can't simply remove it.

A structural wall (if you are indeed going to take it out) has to have its ceiling shored up with a beam that will take the load that the wall used to take. But this is time-consuming work. Before you take out a structural wall, make sure it is worth the effort in terms of your overall plan.

OK, how do you tell? Well, a structural wall is one that holds up beam *ends*. If a beam ends atop a wall, then the wall bears weight. You can sometimes get a look by using a flashlight in the attic. But if unsure, it is worth getting an opinion from a contractor.

The House Beautiful

Whatever you do, don't get into "the *House Beautiful* syndrome." Don't try to make the average-looking house worthy of showing in a decorator magazine. There is no way that most recycles will stand that kind of material costs, and still make a profit.

There are exceptions; when I do a mansion, I make it fit for *House Beautiful*. But anyone who buys a mansion can afford to pay for the beauty.

The average house buyer is satisfied with bright, lean, functional decorating and design. There is no sense giving your future customer a lot of expensive carpet and wallpaper that he or she is not going to want to pay for in the final price of the house. The house has to come in at a price that makes it attractive to the customer, given the kind of neighborhood that it is. If you overdesign and overdecorate, you have a tough time getting the profit out.

What Not To Do In a House

One house I recycled had a somewhat narrow staircase, serviceable but not very good design. I decided to replace the staircase, but it cost me a month. It was an emotional response to the fact that I did not like narrow stairs. The new (wider) stairs did not raise the value of the house one iota, in the rather average-income, white-collar neighborhood. (In another location, a wider stair would have been necessary.) And then I decided to put up pine paneling. Again, this was not the neighborhood for that. More money wasted.

What To Do Right In a House

Let me work a few examples (from my later career) in here that show what a house design can do. At 32 Riverdale, the house was a rundown two-family dwelling. I took out the hall downstairs to make a dining area that had not been there before. The kitchen became a second bedroom. An outdated washroom became a new kitchen. I put the laundry machines down in the basement, which was airy and dry. Upstairs, I removed a hall and installed large windows so that you could see the bay from the whole floor. The Riverdale rent doubled, and so did the market value of the house.

At 5 Griffin, the fifth recycle I worked on, the idea of finding space paid off. The attic was converted into four bedrooms. What had been a cramped two-family house, renting for a total of $275 a month, now became a fine two-family rental giving out $1000 a month. Obviously, creating a two-family house is likely to pay off more handsomely than improving a single-family dwelling. So look for the opportunity.

One Riverview Avenue was a small house (only fifteen by thirty). I removed all walls except around the bedroom to form a huge living-dining-kitchen area. Again, the rent and market value doubled.

At 12 Main Street, the recycle design converted a side porch into a bedroom-den. The rent went from a modest $200 a month to a much richer (in those days) $500.

So much for Step 5, making recycle plans. Let's go on to the next step.

8
Blazing a Paper Trail for Fast Recycling

Step 6 of the recycle is making the paper trail. "Continuity on paper" means that you have a fairly complete written record of your recycle—enough to avoid the hassles that cost time and aggravation, and even spoil a deal. This is "blazing a paper trail."

Think of the delays and extra work if you were unable to produce a deed or a title document or an occupancy permit. The minute you start a recycle, start a "recycle file" rather than throwing the papers helter-skelter onto a shelf.

Headings for the File

Your file should contain a number of folders, each with a heading such as "Negotiations for Sale," and "Contract of Sale," "Correspondence with Lawyer," "Insurance Matters," "Tax Accountant," and so on. Each of these folders then contains related papers that can easily be glanced over to ascertain the state of a particular matter, whether it's your application and acceptance for a certain type of insurance, or a series of typed or handwritten notes on redesign.

Keep a record of your phone conversations. A record can be a jotted memo: "Called Real Estate Broker Smith and told him I was willing to bid $80,000 on Durand Street, January 12, 1981." A memo like this will often be just what you want to refresh your mind when you call Broker Smith—for example—to ask what happened, you haven't heard from him. And Broker Smith says, "Well $55,000 sounded too low." You can then say, "I have a note here that I bid $80,000." You are solidly sure you are right because you wrote down the phone conversation.

If people find you have organized, reliable records and are unwilling to put up with slipshod procedures, they will respect you as a business person. (Conversely they'll give little respect if they think you are running an operation out of your hip pocket.)

Let's say that you write a letter to an insurance company stating, "Per our phone conversation today I am covered in respect to fire and theft up to a limit of $50,000 on an interim basis until we can sign the proper forms. I am awaiting arrival of the forms." If you have a fire before the forms arrive, you have solid evidence from your own carbon copy that you are indeed covered by the company. Otherwise, the insurance agent may not correctly remember that he assured you that you were covered in the interim. Human memory tends to remember the most convenient set of facts.

Lawyers and Time and Paper

A lawyer is supposed to make the right thing happen at the right time. All lawyers are busy. Take the attitude that *you* will be responsible (in the final analysis) for all the legal things getting done in the right way at the right time.

If you are buying a house, in order to get the deal closed and your recycle on the road, get your lawyer to give you a schedule of *what* should happen *when*. Then you can (at the beginning of any given week) pick the schedule out of the file to see where you are, what remains to be done, and when it needs to be done. It's a real worry-saver.

Your relationship with a lawyer depends a great deal on how you present yourself. If you seem unconcerned with bringing things off in good season, the lawyer may put you down as someone he *can* delegate to next week (every day your lawyer has to put *someone* off).

Be organized. Jog the lawyer when it is time to make another step. If need be, run a paper down to the proper authority yourself. Keep the momentum of the recycle going.

Renting-the-Recycle Paperwork

Even though you can buy comprehensive rental agreement forms, you need your lawyer's advice on special local circumstances: the kinds of problems that can crop up, and how to head them off.

If he's a good lawyer, he will advise you in general not to give the tenant any surprises. If there are problems, be frank with the tenant. If you trap a tenant into a bad situation, the tenant can make your life miserable. You can bring a tenant to court but the cost in time and money is high. So, no surprises.

Any important phone conversation that you have with a tenant ought to be recorded by memo. Send the original to him with a carbon for your files. Just mail him a friendly note saying, for example, "Just to confirm our conversation of last night, you have agreed to an increase of $5 a month to cover the increased price of heating oil. The lease will therefore be renewed next April at no more than a 10 percent increase."

That makes it clear to him what you understood the conversation to mean. Now he has, if he disagrees with your version, a chance to register that before it becomes an angry situation.

Planning and Zoning Hearings

Most towns and cities have "zoning laws," or general restrictions and rules to specify the types of housing that can occupy given areas. In some states, the towns have to abide by a statewide set of zoning guidelines; in other states it is entirely up to the local government itself. The purpose of zoning is to have urban development with a coherent plan, rather than a higgedly-piggedly growth: a store next to an apartment next to a garage next to a garbage dump. Thus, zoning goes by "uses," relegating residential freestanding homes to one area, apartments to another (which may overlap), businesses to another, and manufacturing to another. (Sometimes it is desirable to let retail business mix with residences, and so on.)

In theory, having an overall plan for a town is hard to argue with. What is arguable is the application of the law. This is determined by a zoning and planning board made up of citizens.

Have a lawyer represent you who knows what goes on in the town. He will know the people on the board professionally or personally and the board's history of variance-giving. If the lawyer has obtained variances for clients in similar situations, it is very likely that the board will go along this time, too.

Building Code Paperwork

Paperwork for a zoning variance is usually rather minimal, consisting of a petition and reasons. If, however, you are doing major restructuring of a house, you need to do much more detailed and voluminous paperwork. A "plan for reconstruction," has to be presented and approved by the town's department of buildings and construction.

The plan will have a visual (a formal drawing) as well as verbal presentation. All the changes in the house have to follow the specifications of the town's building code, which may call for studs (wall supports) of a certain size and spacing in any newly built section of the house, for a certain minimum insulation, and specify which kind of materials have to be used for roofing.

You don't need to hire an architect for a simple exterior change, such as the addition of a porch. But if you redo the inside completely (that is, "gut" the house, or make big exterior changes), you certainly should consult an architect or an engineer, at least (certainly a good carpenter), concerning how it can be most economically done and how to meet the building codes. Otherwise, your plan is not going to be acceptable to the building inspector and it will have to be redone. That takes up precious time.

Your lawyer may know a local architect or civil engineer who has done business with the building inspector's office and will know the fastest way to get a plan drawn and approved.

The plan and its approval is something you need to photocopy and file. Photocopy everything before you give it to the local bureaucracy. There is no guarantee that *they* can find it when *you* need it. But you will have your own copy.

Anytime you have a conversation with the building inspector that involves a decision to vary the plan, make a memo and mail it to him and keep a carbon.

Once your plan is approved, you get a building permit that allows you to proceed. At the conclusion of the reconstruction, you apply for a certificate of occupancy to allow you to legally sell the house or rent it. (The certificate is another thing you need to have in your files: The person you buy the house from cannot pass on to you his certificate. After buying, you may have to do minimal repair, before the house is eligible for a new certificate of occupancy, even if people were already living there when you bought the place.)

The Buildings List

The office of the inspector of buildings in every town or city has a list of the residences in the town specifying the owner of record and whether or not the building is legally a single or multiple dwelling and what authorized changes have been made in the house. You always look a house up on this list before you go for your closing. The house may feature an unauthorized, "mother-in-law" apartment: You can rent it to your immediate family but not legally to unrelated tenants.

You may find that the building has been enlarged without

permit, and so on, all problems that take time to straighten out. Check first, then you won't have to go after the seller later. Getting a reduction in the price at the closing is easier than chasing the seller afterward.

The Building Inspector

Let us assume now that the building is "legal," your remodeling plan is approved, and the building permit in order. An inspector from the town office will come by from time to time to see that you are following the plan, meeting specifications.

The inspector is usually a civil engineer (or at least a very experienced builder) and he may have some very sound and useful advice. I make it a point to be pleasant and cooperative. The building inspector can revoke your permit and stop the recycle dead if he feels that you are not following the plan. (In case you find the inspector is not being reasonable, consult your lawyer. Do not take things into your own hands. Do not ignore the inspector's decisions. It is very expensive to tear down and rebuild.)

OK, this leaves us with three last "paper-trail" subjects.

The first is the question of financial records.

Setting Up an Accounting System

You can drive yourself crazy with double-entry bookkeeping, or you can do it the easy way. You can do it right out of a special checkbook used for the recycle with every recycle transaction recorded in it.

If you get cash from Uncle Fred as a contribution toward making your recycle more luxurious, don't take the cash from Uncle Fred and buy bricks with it, deposit the cash in your special checkbook so that there is a record of it coming in as well as going out. If you sell your stocks to help finance the recycle, don't hand the cash over to the furnace installer. Put the cash in your account first and pay *everything* by check.

Thus, come tax time, you have a record of all the ins and outs. You have a record for your accountant (who helps you make out your income tax) and a record in case you are audited by the Internal Revenue. The auditor will relax when he sees your accounts are in order.

Getting an Accountant

Before you get very far into a recycle, hire an accountant to do your taxes. Even if tax-paying time is still eight months away, there are some very specific advantages in recycling that you need to know as you begin the recycle so you can take advantage of them.

Keep the bills filed alphabetically and marked with the check number by which they were paid. Have them all set up for your accountant to total when he makes up your business expense sheet on the income tax form.

Can't you do the tax work without getting an accountant? Sure, but unless you are up-to-date on accounting methods and the latest rulings of the Internal Revenue Service on what is and what is not deductible as legitimate expenses (and, believe me, that can change from year to year), then you may be getting into hot water even with the most innocent of intentions. And an accountant will advise you on the best way to "depreciate" your house for tax purposes. A house can be depreciated over twenty years or thirty years or fifty years. Each will have an advantage for a given situation.

The accountant will advise you on how to proceed so your profits are taxed under long-term capital gains at a low rate. In other words, an accountant will pay for himself in a very short time.

Keep one set of tax records on file with the accountant and another copy in your file. Send the originals to the IRS. The only thing that you can lose in a fire is one copy. (After five years, except in case of fraud, you cannot be held liable for back taxes; so you don't need to keep files forever.)

Insurance on the Paper Trail

Insurance protects you at low cost against the kind of catastrophe that has a high cost: fire loss, theft loss, and personal injury suits. The best way is to get a local insurance agent. Ask around for one with a good reputation. He will place the insurance in a way that is advantageous. He also has some leverage with the insurance companies if he is a good agent, because he wants his clients paid off when they deserve it. Insurance companies like to keep a good agent happy.

Personal injury suits involving awards of a million or two million dollars are not that uncommon. The homeowners policy does not cover more than $100,000 to $200,000 in personal injuries, so get "umbrella insurance" (not only for the house, but for your auto insurance, etc.). It covers the difference between the "normal" award for personal injury and the extraordinary million dollar award that can sometimes be given in the case of permanently disabling injuries.

If you have lots of high-priced valuables, it is worth getting them appraised. It is very hard to prove the value of something that has disappeared.

Keep all your correspondence and receipts for insurance policies and premiums. Even an insurance company can have a fire in its office.

Real Estate Broker Dealings

More houses are sold through brokers than through sales directly between individuals. A good broker is someone who can pair up houses and people. The good broker is a time-saver; he keeps you from going to see things that you would never buy, and steers you to things that you will likely want to buy. The broker is technically on the side of the seller as the agent *of* the seller, but a smart broker also wants the approval and trust of the buyer.

A broker is a salesman, usually not above "puffing" the property to persuade you to do something that (in the light of sober reflection) you will regret. The more grandiose the broker's claims, the greater ought to be your skepticism.

Just because you have *said* you will buy a house, there is no legal compulsion to go through with it. The broker knows (and you should know) that the only legally binding deal in real estate is one that is in writing. So, you are *not* committed until you sign the papers.

In other kinds of agreements, say if you tell someone you will buy his antique rocker for $500, and he accepts verbally, you have a legal contract. The courts will enforce it. In real estate, "Saying doesn't make it so. Signing makes it so." Keep all signed papers in your file.

And with that, we have completed Step 6, the blazing of the paper trail. The next four chapters cover Steps 7 and 8, in which we recycle the house's systems (plumbing, etc.) and the house itself (interiors, exterior, etc.).

9

Being Your Own Contractor to Build Up Recycle Profit

When it comes to recycling the systems, such as plumbing and heating, and in recycling the exterior and interior of the house itself, you have to choose between doing it yourself and hiring others to do it. There ought to be no ego involved here. Just because you can do a great job reroofing, for instance, don't let that trap you into doing it if you can get the roof put on quickly and cheaply by professional roofers while you spend your time on other urgently needed work. (Reroofing is one of the things that is relatively cheap and safe to contract out to another set of hands.)

Hire only when hiring will save *both* time and money, or when you are not an expert and don't have that much time to become one. The "meter" is always running: If you are paying $1000 a month in interest, you save $1000 by finishing a month earlier. It is simple arithmetic. You can't halt the interest charges *until* you finish the house and sell it. The earlier you finish, the more money you save.

And now, let's look at what it means to "contract out." You can "let a contract" for any or all of the work in a recycle. That is, you can not only contract to hire electricians and plumbers and carpenters, but you can contract with someone to hire and supervise everyone and everything, so that you don't even have to be there.

You can always balance the cost of help against the cost of interest. If you can hire someone to do a job that will shorten the recycle time by a month, and you're paying $1,000 interest on your loans every month, then you can subtract in your mind, the $1,000 from the amount you have to pay.

Contracting Profit and Recycling Profit

When you hire a general contractor, the usual fee is 20 percent of the cost. If your house recycle material and labor costs $20,000, the general contractor takes another $4000 as his fee.

Obviously that is a big slice out of the recycling profit which the recycler saves if he acts as his own general contractor. So, normally, the recycler does the overall supervision and takes responsibility for the synchronizing of the electrical work, plumbing, carpentry, (etc.) *and* the supervising of all of this.

Thus, if the recycler decides to *subcontract* the electrical work rather than do it himself, he puts the job up for bid and gets three or four electricians to submit estimates for the work. Then he picks the one whose reputation and price make the best deal.

I have had as many as eight people working for me on a house: two day laborers doing simple nailing jobs, two experienced carpenters doing more difficult work, one plasterer working inside, two plumbers on a plumbing subcontract, and a house painter working by the day on the exterior trim. This was an unusual situation in which I had a firm buyer for the house who wanted it promptly and who was willing to pay my price. Weighing the wages against the possibility of doing those jobs myself, I decided that I was much better off subcontracting the work.

Generally, I prefer to do as much as I can myself. In a more usual recycle I would have painted the trim, plastered, and done most of the carpentry myself (taken it as far as I could with my own hands before letting more expert help come in). My wages are the extra profits I get by saving on help.

Hiring Is Not Always the Answer

A man for hire is not your partner, whether he works fast or slow, he gets the same wage, usually. Alternatively, if he is a subcontractor he gets a fixed price for the entire job. So you lose either in time or in money when you hire by the hour or subcontract the work (as compared to doing it yourself).

There is no sense being caught up in fantasy; if you can't do it, and there is no time to learn, then you have no choice but hire or subcontract. But you *can* learn how to do an amazing number of things: simple plumbing, insulating, electrical layout. You can do all of these things, if you commit to finding out how to do them, and are not afraid to plunge in, get your hands dirty, and make mistakes.

The hiring trap: You spend your time running around telling people how to do things that you could just as quickly do yourself. On the other hand, if you can hire someone at say $3 to $5 an hour (to do the hauling, cleaning, picking up, and simple nailing), so that you are free to do more complex things and to plan the work, then it is certainly worth it.

A friend of mine did a little gentlemanly recycling one year: He "built a house by telephone," leaving most of the work to others. He found that when he added up his costs at the end (he should have been adding them all along), he would have to sell the house at about 20 percent above the going market value to make a profit. Of course, he eventually sold at the market price, so he didn't get paid for all his time on the telephone. (Luckily my friend was well off and could afford to lose his profit without cramping his lifestyle. Most of us are not that fortunate.)

Using Day-By-Day-Planning to Recycle

A recycler not only has to keep track of costs day by day, but keep track of what has been done, what needs to be done, and what materials and manpower and machines (if any) are going to have to be on hand to do it.

I keep a pad and pencil in my pocket and make notes all day long. If I am out of white paint, I note "10 g wh pt" and make sure I get it from the store before it closes that evening. If I am ready for the window man, I put "call win man" on the pad and get to him that evening. One of my co-workers once complained, "Every night, we go home with a three-page list." But that is exactly what makes a recycle pay off. Time is money. If you stand around twiddling your thumbs while the hardware store runs ten gallons of paint out to you because you forgot to order it, you are having an expensive twiddle.

This kind of planning doubles in importance if you hire by the hour: You have to have laid out beforehand all the jobs you want done and have the materials on hand to do them. Once the hired men arrive, the clock is running. And you want their hands busy.

Even when you have hired, explained, and supplied the things needed, you still have to be on your toes. The intelligence level of the people you hire varies from genius to somewhat lower than that. I once was away from a recycle for two days and came back to find the laborers had taken down the wrong interior wall. Another time, one inexperienced hand installed a door upside down. (He had never really *noticed* how doors ought to look.) It's sort of amusing when it happens, but enough of that and you find you *aren't* laughing all the way to the bank.

Union Work Versus Nonunion Work

This can be a touchy subject in theory, but in practice, unions are not all that interested in having their members work on small jobs such as recycling a single house. Unions are busy getting the "big ones" nailed down: condos, hotels, and commercial buildings. They are not going to bother with the recycler who is, in their view, small potatoes. Legally speaking, no union can force you to hire union workers, but it can make things mighty unpleasant for you if you don't by picketing and harassment. As a recycler, however, you are probably not worth the trouble.

The most satisfactory help I get comes from beginning recyclers. They work for pay in my current recycle in between bouts with their own house. This is motivated help. And two recyclers can derive mutual benefit by starting houses at the same time and trading help back and forth as their projects progress, each learning from the other.

Salvaging a Recycling Profit

The other great advantage of acting as your own general contractor and/or subcontractor is that you can find bargain goods by using a little ingenuity. In general, this kind of bargain comes under the heading of "salvage," that is, goods meant for or used by somebody else. These goods are available because they have been misdirected, mismanufactured, or used and put up for resale. "Recycling profit" doesn't come from some bold master stroke, but from patient bargain hunting. With each bargain your recycling profit is compounded.

Where will you find the best bargains? First and foremost at the flea markets. A flea market is simply an area where people with goods to sell can come, set up temporary shop, and sell their wares. At day's end or at the end of the weekend, they pack it all up again and off they go, leaving bare grounds again. It's a sort of "used/new" bargain fair.

Flea markets feature both "pro" and "amateur" sellers. Some make a living selling their wares; others just go to get rid of a few things, make a few pennies, and have a good time socializing and bargaining. You can usually get whatever is there for half the retail price (maximum), on down to ten or even one percent of new value.

At the huge Englishtown, N.J., flea market (where I most often go), I have found doors, shutters, plywood siding, roofing paper, light fixtures, furniture, window frames. When I am recycling, I get up every weekend morning at 5:45 A.M. and get to the flea market when it opens. I always find fantastic bargains. But one key to shopping these markets: Don't buy something "for later on." Buy what you *know* you can use *now*, and let the rest stay right where it is.

There are several other sources for bargains:

- fire sales
- classified ads
- church sales
- lawn and garage sales
- thrift stores
- auctions
- factory seconds
- pawn shops
- pennysaver newspapers (full of ads for goods)

After you have been recycling for a while, you will discover more and more bargain sources. Read the newspapers, ask around, talk to other recyclers you meet. Buying bargains is one very sure way of maximizing your recycling profit.

To identify true bargains once you locate sources, you really need to know the market price of the things you are buying. Otherwise you can go to a lot of trouble to get something that's no real bargain. Some sellers advertise their goods only slightly off regular market price. Bargain hunting is only worthwhile if you buy at half the retail price or less. Even if one purchase turns out to be defective or not as sturdy as it looked, the money saved on real bargains more than makes up for it.

10

Tools for Fun and Profit in the 1980s Recycle

The way the recycler uses tools differs considerably from the way the home hobbyist uses tools. The difference is a difference in philosophy. Usually, the home carpenter is making highly finished pieces: bookshelves, counter tables, window benches. His aim is to make something beautiful that enhances the comfort and look of the house.

The recycler is much more utilitarian. He does very little building-in. In order to attract a wider range of buyers, the recycler leaves decorating-type changes to the individual taste of the buyer. (If you show a family with kids a bachelor's built-in hideaway bar and wine-cellar dining alcove, you are not making much of a positive impression. The family might want to rip it out.) The focus is on simple repair: making doorframes whole, shoring up ceilings, taking down or building interior walls to create a more spacious feeling.

The recycler asks how cheaply can he buy his tools. He needs plenty of cheap hammers, pliers, crowbars, and screwdrivers. He wants to be able to lose or break them without weeping. He doesn't want to buy top-of-the-line tools. He wants to make the tool pay its way, use it till it is worn out and then discard it. The home-shop hobbyist, on the other hand, does not see the cost of tools as a profit/loss concern.

A usual home shop is designed around heavy, stationary precision power tools, such as a drill press, lathe, and bench saw. But a recycler's power tools are portable: portable power saw, handheld drills, disc sanders, staple guns. The recycler's house is the recycler's "shop." He stores the tools at the job, if they are secure, if not, in a locked tool box in the car.

I have never had a home shop where I did precision work. It is so seldom called for in recycling that there is no need for a home shop. If you have a precision job, you can farm it out to a cabinetmaker.

Wear and Tear on Tools

The recycler is working against time—not hurriedly, but certainly efficiently. Time is money, so he makes every work minute count. He does not run out to buy exactly the right tool if he can make do with the tool at hand, even though it may mean bending or breaking it. He may use a sabersaw when ideally he would have a circular saw, and he uses pliers when a wrench is called for, all to save time.

The recycler does with fewer tools and makes them serve more purposes. He wants to make it through the day with the tools he has available, if at all possible. Time saved is money made. Jokingly, I used to say that I recycled the first house with a jigsaw. As a matter of fact, I had a wrench, a hammer, a couple of screwdrivers, and not much more. If I couldn't get it done with the tools I had, I improvised a way. I had to because I had no money.

This approach means more wear and tear on tools. There is no way you can use tools hard and keep them looking like new. But as a recycler, the appearance of your tools is of little concern; they are only a means to an end: a profitable recycle for you.

Buying on the Cheap

A flea market is one place to find lots of older kinds of tools inexpensively. You can buy a hand bit and drills for a couple of bucks, which will do the job of a $50 power drill (provided you don't have to make a precision fit). I once even got myself a bench band saw for $15, which I carted around to the work site if I needed to make curved cuts on anything.

Old house auctions are another source for marvelous tools such as wood clamps and two-man saws (stuff that can be used in rough work that comes up during most recycles). Actually, I have gotten quite knowledgeable about "antique" tools if only because I use them as a matter of course.

A "casual attitude toward tools" doesn't mean ignorance. I have spent a good deal of time, as should every recycler, reading up on tool types and their functions. The books that I like the most are *The Incredible Illustrated Tool Book* (Pathmark, Boston) and *Tools and Their Uses* (Dover, New York). Both use the pictures from a Navy training manual and the illustrations are very clear.

Now I know enough to buy sensibly, if cheaply. I know what tools there are to *be* bought and how they work. If there is a specialized tool that really saves time, I do not hesitate to buy it. If I need a bolt cutter to lop off the heads of bolts in my recycling, I get one. I don't fool around for hours trying to hacksaw my way through the job.

Save-Time Safety Practices

The biggest time-waster in the world is injury. It is a real concern to a recycler who is depending on his own hands to do the work. You can take some very simple safety precautions that will keep your recycle humming along uninterrupted by accidents.

The most common working injury is caused by nails: either stepping on one or being cut by one's sharp end. You can avoid a foot injury from nails by wearing thick-soled shoes. Even better, have a "nail barrel" to throw all nail discards into; then you won't step on them.

Cuts from nails occur when you fail to remove a nail from a board and it sticks out like a little spear. Before you throw a board away, remove or bend over all nails. If you see a nail sticking out from a board, *always* take the time to bend the nail over and into the wood.

Another cause of frequent injury is the ladder. I always prefer to spend a little more and get an aluminum ladder. A wood ladder can break unexpectedly causing an accident. If you must use a wood ladder in a recycle, lay it on the floor and step on each rung hard enough to see that each is solid. Injuries involving ladders and heights are inexcusable. Take your time when you are at heights over three inches off the floor.

Now about electricity, which is the one no-foolin' deadly companion of all recyclers. Even a mild 110 volt shock can jolt your heart to a standstill if you happen to be unlucky. *But* if you happen to be standing on something wet that penetrates your shoes, the shock will not be mild, it will rip right through you and at least knock you out. When your feet are damp, you act as an electrical wire to any electricity that short-circuits from your power tools onto your body. So, don't get wet feet. If you do, stop working and put some dry shoes on.

There is a "GFI" or "ground fault interrupter" that works much more quickly to cut off the current than a fuse can. It's a good investment in your own life to have your own GFI and use it with power tools, even if it is a bit of a nuisance to carry around.

Saving Eyes and Lungs and Hands

The one thing I carry around is a pair of nonprescription, unbreakable plastic glasses, which I put on whenever I use a circular saw, or when painting overhead or mixing chemicals that could injure my eyes if splashed. The glasses offer plenty of protection to the vulnerable, irreplaceable eyes, the only pair you are going to be given.

When I am power sanding, or floor sanding, I put on a nose cone just to keep the particles out of my lungs. There is a biological lung defense mechanism against particles, but why overload it? The same when scraping off paint: Lots of old paint has very poisonous lead in it. Be especially careful when spray painting, as it is hazardous to your lungs. Always wear a cone mask when you scrape old paint.

Nothing gets sorer when I work than my hands. On rough jobs, I wear work gloves. An infected scar on your hand resulting from your not wearing gloves yesterday makes working torture, today.

To sum it up, recycling is not a macho game where you court injury for the sake of appearance. There is nothing macho about getting hurt and losing money because your recycle was delayed.

Efficiency Through Organizing

The most time-wasting occupation in recycling is looking for tools that were here a couple of days ago. To avoid that, take a half hour at the end of your work day to clean up the area. Pick everything up off the floor, set tools back in storage bins or boxes and sweep the floor to pick up any stray tools lying in the litter. Sweep the litter into a waste container, so that you are not continually stumbling over little wood bits or skidding in the sawdust or slipping on a paint can lid.

An inexpensive and easy way to store tools is in a series of labeled rubber buckets. Every big power tool can have its own bucket. One bucket can hold turpentine cans or other paint thinner. The brushes, cleaned with thinner, can be locked into mason jars with a little thinner in the bottom to stay moist and ready to use for months.

Most of my painting is done with rollers, and not brushes. Let the roller sit in paint thinner in its pan overnight, then throw it away when done. A little thinner every night keeps a roller going for weeks. Use a new one for your next project.

Working with Effect

One thing you can never have too many of is pockets. Get a carpenter's apron and carry in it the various things you use every day. You can nail faster from an apron pocket than any other way.

It pays to organize materials as well as tools. I usually have long pieces of unused lumber in one pile and short scrap lumber in another, plus a pile for metal scrap.

Efficiency of motion is not the kind of thing that you can graft onto your work at the end of the day. The more time and energy efficient you are, the more profit you will have at the end of the recycle.

Tool Maintenance

Even though you do treat your tools casually, they can stand a little care. The electric grinding wheel is the one bench tool that is really handy to have (always wear glasses when using it). If your wood chisel is dull, you waste a lot of time trying to work with it. If your claw hammer face is rounded instead of flat, you don't hit nails as true.

Besides sharpening tools, you must lubricate them. Even if you got your electric drill cheaply, you can still put a drop or two of oil into the proper holes when you begin the week. In fact, you can set aside the first few minutes on Monday as "lube hour." That will prevent burnouts during the week. In addition to household oil, you need to have on hand some penetrating oil to loosen any rust, and a six pack of WD 40, which is a spray that drives off water and keeps a damp tool from rusting overnight.

Suppose that you do lose a tool you need (and can't duplicate) down a crack or between the walls? You can rescue that tool with several sorts of mechanical tweezers equipped with a sort of a dentist's inspection mirror on a stick. With that and a flashlight you can rescue any object from the darkest crevice. And if it is a long drop, have a good solid block magnet on a string to drop down the crevice. It should pull the thing right back out.

The purpose of tools is to serve the recycler, to make his work go quickly and efficiently so that the profit of his labor will be maximized. He works hard recycling and deserves every penny he can get from it.

part IV

Maximizing Profit on the All-Important House

11

Inexpensive Insulation for Maximum Energy Savings

Step 7 of the nine recycling steps involves redoing, whenever necessary, the "house systems": insulation, heating, plumbing, and electricity. In the ideal recycle all these systems are in place, but reality is never ideal. *Some* work, on at least one of the systems, is usually required in any recycle.

The complete redo of any system is expensive. Have a subcontractor (electrician, plumber, etc.) evaluate the situation and submit an estimate on repairing the system before you decide whether or not to tackle it yourself.

The Order of Interior and Exterior Work

The order in which you tackle the recycle work is very important. For instance, on the exterior part of the recycle, you do roof, windows, and siding first; awnings, fences, and landscapes last. Here is the most efficient order in which to do the work:

1. Reroof first. The new roof protects the interior.
2. Replace windows and exterior doors.
3. Install new siding as soon as weather permits.
4. Do plumbing work prior to room interiors.
5. Insulate roof and walls.
6. Repair interior ceilings.
7. Repair interior walls.
8. Repair interior floors.
9. Install awnings, fences, and other exterior decorative effects.
10. Do landscaping.

The Insulation System Functions

The first system we will look at is insulation, known more elaborately as "weatherproofing." The function of the system is to slow down (no one can completely stop it) the transfer of energy through the roof and walls of the house: from the inside to the outside during the winter, and from the outside to the inside during the summer. Slowing the transfer of heat equals good heating efficiency and keeps the house cool even when you don't use air conditioning.

There is one thing that any canny buyer will ask and that is "How much does it cost to heat the house?" He may even ask for last winter's fuel bills to prove it.

A recycler is concerned with the same question: High fuel bills mean the house needs reinsulation, and that means expense. It also means that there's a profitable *need* to be filled.

Most houses more than five years old have insufficient insulation. The cost of fuel today is so much more than it was a few years ago that it pays to put in much heavier insulation. Added insulation can pay for itself in three to ten years, and that is a good pay-off. (A well-insulated house is a great selling point, for the same reason.) Insulation costs vary wildly depending on where you add insulation and how extensively. Reinsulating the attic and basement can cost a few hundred dollars while reinsulating the *walls* (of an already-constructed house) is much more expensive.

Today there is often a tax incentive program offered by the federal, state, and/or local government, which helps pay the cost.

Insulating the Attic Pays Off

The addition of insulation in the attic pays off better than anywhere else in the house because heat rises. If allowed to, it will leak speedily through the uninsulated roof.

There are three ways to insulate an attic: (1) insulating the floor of the attic, leaving the attic ceiling unfinished; (2) insulating the attic roof to the peak, which is more effective; (3) insulating an installed "false ceiling" under the roof peak, which is the most effective of all.

You might think that insulating all three ways would give the best effect, but sufficient insulation in any one of those places is all good efficiency requires.

What is sufficient insulation? Insulation texts will give you an "R" value for insulation sufficient for your particular latitude. (The R value called for in the state of Maine is more than double that called for in the state of Georgia, for example.)

There are a number of types of insulation, each with its own R value per inch of thickness. Just briefly, all insulating materials are either *foam, fiber,* or *fill.* Foam (which usually has to be applied professionally) has two to three times the R value of fiber or fill.

Doing It Versus Having It Done

Let's say your house needs its attic insulated and you call in a professional and he gives you a figure for the job. It's more than your budget for materials and outside labor will allow. So you decide to do it yourself. In this case, fiber, not fill or foam, is the answer. Fiber is the cheapest and easiest to install. Fill is loose stuff, requiring a ceiling or wall to contain it. Foam is for pros.

Fiberglass is the most widely available fiber, the cheapest, and the easiest to put in. Nine times out of ten, a recycler insulates with fiberglass rolls or batts.

To insulate the roof, you nail the rolls or batts between the two-by-four rafters. Cut the fiberglass to fit exactly between rafters. If you are insulating the floor, fit the rolls between the floor joists. The more closely you fit the space, the less heat escapes through the roof.

The Moisture Problem Licked

Every house has two requirements for effective insulation: first, to keep heat from passing through the roof and walls; second, to keep moisture from condensing on the insulation or against the ceiling or roof.

You keep heat *in* by stopping air flow; you keep moisture from condensing by promoting air flow. So it is a compromise. Warm air rises from the lower floors of the house. It picks up moisture; the warmer the air, the greater the moisture content. One of four things happens: (1) The moist air is prevented from reaching the attic. (2) The moist air hits the colder insulation fibers and drops its moisture on these fibers (robbing them of most of their insulating properties). (3) The moist air hits the cold underside of the roof and condenses on that surface, rotting the wood. (4) The moist air is allowed to escape through the roof beam or attic vents, but not in such volume as to cause a great heat loss.

Obviously you want to prevent (2) and (3) and make (1) or (4) happen. If you insulate the floor of the attic, you go for (1).

Insulating the Roof and Basement

Each fiberglass roll has a shiny aluminum facing—the vapor barrier. Place that aluminum face down on the attic floor to keep the moisture from rising up into the attic. It then also obviously keeps moisture out of the insulation fibers.

Suppose you decide to insulate the *roof* of the attic, instead of the *floor*, because that is more efficient, or because you want to finish off the attic some day as a spare set of rooms. Then you go for (4), letting the air and moisture escape.

To do that, you hang the insulation between the rafters with the bright vapor barrier face *toward* the room, so that you can see it when you have finished fastening the roll in place. This keeps the moisture from going into the fibers. But you have to (1) allow the air to escape through one or more attic *vents*, and (2) let the ridge beam "breathe."

Vents are louvres designed to let air out slowly. One in each end of the attic will do the trick. To let the ridge beam breathe, fasten the upper edges of the rolls just short of the ridge beam, so that the warm moist air that has not gone out the vents can be absorbed by the ridge beam and transmitted through the beam to the outside.

Sometimes you may have to add a ridge vent as well to allow air to escape more rapidly. If the ridge beam or other surface has started to show surface rot, then you need a ridge vent.

The second most frequent culprit in heat loss is the basement. Very few people bother to insulate it, and yet the basement, with its cement walls, is constantly losing heat.

You can insulate the basement by first hanging fiberglass rolls in the basement ceiling, vapor barriers facing down toward you. Second, you can nail furring strips to the inside walls of the basement and hang solid foam insulating board on the strips covering the foam boards in turn with wallboard for fireproofing. (Foam insulating board is flammable.) This will make your basement considerably warmer. You don't have to worry about insulating the floor because the floor is deep enough in the ground to stay fairly warm, year 'round.

Insulating Walls

If the house walls have some but not much insulation at all, leave the walls alone; it is an expensive job. But *if* there is no insulation (as is the case with many Victorian houses) you will have to insulate.

You can either hire a professional to blow in cellulose or inject foam insulation. Or, you can figure out how to insulate it yourself.

About the only way to insulate a wall yourself is to use an insulating fill, such as vermiculite, which comes in bags and can be taken to the attic and emptied down between the wall studs to fill up the space from there.

If your house is two-story, your second floor probably will prevent the fill from filling up the first floor wall spaces. You must then go outside, remove the siding at the second floor level, cut a hole in the sheathing, and drop the vermiculite down until it fills the first floor spaces between the wall studs.

Cutting Loss Through the Siding

Once you've dropped the insulation inside, you want to keep the cold air from getting into the insulating fill. Check out the siding of the house to make sure that it doesn't have a lot of cracks in it. If you do spot cracks, caulk them with an appropriate material.

The only remaining alternative is to remove the interior wall and hang fiberglass. If you are of a mind to remove the interior wall anyway (because it's so badly cracked and unfixable) then, as far as insulating goes, it is the ideal solution. Hanging fiberglass works well because it provides vapor barrier and all.

Cutting Heat Loss through Windows

Rather than tearing out the interior walls, it might be much more productive to spend a fraction of that time sealing the windows. Window leaks cause much of the heat loss in any house. There are two ways you can go about this. You can buy insulating strips for this purpose or use the Weir Special Window Sealing Technique: Caulk the upper sash of the window in place (you never open it anyway). Make sure there are no chinks left for air currents to wander through. Then weatherstrip the four sides of the lower sash (the vertical sides with commercial stripping). Insulate the upper horizontal frame by opening the window from the bottom so you can reach the inside face of the lower horizontal of the upper sash; coat that with silicone rubber sealant and cover with a single layer of Saran Wrap. Then close the lower window and let the silicone harden, open it, remove the Saran Wrap and you have a perfect seal of the upper horizontal frame of the lower window.

Do the same for the lower horizontal frame of the lower window: Coat the bottom of the frame with silicone, put Saran Wrap on the window sill, and close the window. Let the silicone harden, open the window, and remove Saran Wrap. Now you have a window that is perfectly sealed against heat leakage.

There is an enormous amount more that can be learned about insulating a house, but the methods in this chapter cover 80 percent of the practical solutions the recycler will need.

Read more, a little bit at a time. Don't try to swallow a whole book on insulation in one evening.

Insulate well: The country's energy crisis calls for every bit of insulation that *can* be economically installed.

12

Making Plumbing Pay Off in the 1980s Recycle

Today's home owner is accustomed to plenty of bathroom space (minimal waiting), lots of hot water with which to shower and bathe, and an automatic laundry and dishwasher, as well as outdoor tap to water the lawn.

This array of "necessities" is relatively recent; older houses usually lack several requirements, and happily so. Nothing upgrades a house more, per dollar spent, than adding bathrooms, dishwashers, laundry facilities—and the plumbing they require.

When you estimate your cost of repair and renovation in an average suburban neighborhood, you have to include the cost of:

- one bathroom for every two bedrooms
- gas or electric hot water heater
- outside taps on all sides of the house where there is much lawn
- a dishwasher and laundry facilities installed

In addition to that, you have to fix the existing plumbing. So when you inspect a house:

- turn each tap on for five minutes; make sure you get clean water through it, that the basins don't overflow, and the taps don't leak when shut off
- flush all toilets to make sure they operate
- turn on one hot water tap for 15 minutes to check the hot water supply

Adding New Plumbing

Decide whether or not you have enough expertise to *estimate the cost* of fixing and adding the needed plumbing. If you have doubts, get a plumber to do it. Some will come to give estimates free; some charge for estimates. (Additionally, your plumber may spot problems your uneducated eye has not spotted, saving you time and trouble later.)

Let's say that the plumber has given you an estimate, but you find it too steep. So you decide to do the work yourself. Your plumbing additions are easy to install if you plan them thoughtfully. The most important time-saver is locating the new plumbing near the existing plumbing because then you need less pipe to connect, less wall to break open.

For instance, if you add a new bathroom, it should be adjacent to your old bathroom. If you add a new washer-drier in the basement, locate it close to the existing incoming (pressure system) pipes *and* outgoing (drain) pipes. That will cut expense and labor considerably.

Plumbing Materials to Use

As we will see later in this chapter, there are various kinds of pipe and various kinds of pipe join-ups (couplings) between pipes. Choosing the right ones will minimize your plumbing renovation costs.

Some tips: *Plastic* pipe is the pipe to choose if you haven't ever worked with plumbing before. It cuts and joins more easily than any other. Next easiest to work with is *copper*. Like plastic, you can get "transition joints" from the old pipe to the new material, from galvanized pipe to plastic, or plastic to copper, etc. The new pipes don't have to be the same material as the old.

Replace deteriorated sections of pipe rather than the whole pipe assembly. It may *look* a bit higgedly-piggedly close up, but pipe is either buried in the walls, out of sight under fixtures, or in the basement.

And now for tools: Special plumbing tools make handling pipe much easier. The most familiar of these is the pipe wrench which has a loose lower jaw that automatically takes the right angle to hold the round shape of the pipe.

Strap wrenches and chain wrenches are used for bigger pieces of pipe, and the basin wrench for working up behind wash basins. To take off the nuts in the plumbing fixtures, you use a regular adjustable wrench, or you use a self-locking "vicegrip" type plier with cloth tucked into the jaw to keep it from scarring the nuts.

Looking at the Plumbing Systems

The naive person looks at plumbing as a single system of pipes, but in fact, any plumbing system is really *three* systems. The first is the system bringing the water in from the outside. That, naturally enough, is known as the *pressure system.*

The pressure system brings the water *to* the appliance or fixture. If it's a wash basin, the pressure system brings the water to the faucets, from the underside.

The drain system takes over *after* you use the water. In a wash basin it begins in the bottom of the basin, where the water drains out. The drains carry the water down into the basement and out of the house into the sewer system or the septic tank. As each drain comes out of the fixture or appliance, it soon takes a *dip,* a U-shaped section. This "trap" lets water go through, but when the water has gone through, some of it stays in the bottom of the U.

The purpose of the trap is to block sewer gas. Each drain

connects to the disposal system of the house. A disposal system, whether sewer or septic tank, generates a great deal of not very pleasant-smelling sewer gas. Sewer gas is also unhealthy. By blocking each drain with water, the traps block out all sewer gas.

The Unknown Vent System

The vent system acts both as a way of keeping the traps functioning and also as a way of letting most of the sewage gas out of the drains. Most people wouldn't recognize a vent system if they saw one, and most everyone sees one. The top of every vent system is one or more little vent pipes with a conical cap sticking up through the roof.

That vent pipe is the top of a "main vent" which goes straight down through the building. Little side vent pipes connect to every trap. If the vent pipe wasn't there, the water coursing down the drain would build up a suction between it and the water remaining in the trap, and that suction would pull all the water *out* of the trap. If that would happen, the sewer gas would float back up into the fixture and into the house. In other words, the house would smell bad.

But since the vent pipe does let air in below the trap, no suction builds up and the water stays in the trap. Furthermore, since the main vent connects directly to the main drain in the cellar, any accumulation of sewer gas in the drain is dispersed into the atmosphere.

Checking Out the Plumbing

Have a house checked out by a plumber if any kind of plumbing problem shows itself during the inspection of a house. Even if you can fix the problem, its existence shows that the plumbing is old and may need thorough checking out to see how big its problems really are.

Let's look first at the *pressure system*. The most frequent problem is leaky faucets. Every faucet has an inside valve mechanism seated on a soft washer which keeps it watertight.

But the washer wears down; it leaks and so does the faucet. Every home repair book (of which literally hundreds are available) shows how to replace a washer. A leaky faucet will cost you little to fix, but it does indicate bad maintenance of the plumbing system.

The second most frequent pressure system problem is a "running toilet," with water constantly trickling out of the overflow pipe in the toilet cabinet and down into the drain. This means that the float valve in the cabinet is not shutting the water off entirely at the end of a flush. This, again, is not usually hard to fix but it does indicate a careless owner.

The third, more serious problem with the supply system is leaks in the joints or pipe somewhere. This has to be fixed or it will flood the house. This kind of leak means replacing the joint or pipe, a job which is not all that simple. But it can be done; you can learn how. But again, a leak in a pipe itself may mean that other pipes are ready to let go.

Drain Problem Spots

Drains carry away the waste and can get plugged up with waste. A clogged drain can usually be cleared without taking the drain apart, but you can never tell. When you inspect a house, if the flush water doesn't clear out from the toilet bowl, or if turning on the sink or wash-basin tap causes the fixture to overflow, then you have a clogged drain somewhere, and again this won't necessarily raise the cost of recycling much, but it does indicate that there may be more serious problems in the plumbing system as a whole.

The majority of clogged drains can be cleared out with a "plumber's helper." Run water into a basin or sink, then pump the rubber suction cup of the plumber's helper to force out the clogged material. If the plumber's helper doesn't do it, then a commercial drain cleaning chemical may do it. Follow carefully the directions on the bottle.

The third thing you can do is buy a "drain snake" at the hardware store, which can be augered down the drain, through the trap (where the clogged material usually lies) to clear out the drain. If this doesn't work, then you have to take the drain apart at the trap, if that is where the blockage is. Or, go down in the basement where the drains funnel into the main drain and open up the cleanout plugs down there. Then use the snake to clear out the blockage in the basement drains.

The Vent Problems

It's easy to detect a vent problem, because the house will have a faint bad odor to it when you walk in—one that is unmistakably like standing over a sewer grate.

In some old houses you may have no vent system, which means that you have to put one in, which is very expensive. You definitely need to get a plumber to estimate costs of a proper vent system.

When you inspect, make sure a house has a vent system. If flushing a toilet makes a horrible gurgle, either there is no venting system or the vent system doesn't work. If you can inspect the roof you can quickly tell whether or not there is a vent system: no stacks, no venting system. If the vent system works except for one or two traps, you can install one-way valves in the traps and solve the problem.

Adding or Replacing Pipe

Plastic is the least expensive and lightest of pipe materials. You make connections by gluing the parts together. Plastic pipe bends easily to curve into the proper position to make a connection. Rigid copper tubing cannot do that.

To add or replace pipe you simply saw through it, glue a coupling on it, and glue the couple to the end of another pipe. You make the joint permanent by applying glue to the ends of pipe (it is really a solvent, which melts the outer layer of pipe and then lets it harden and stick to the coupling).

While the pipe joint hardens, you must support it in place so that it lines up exactly the way you want it. The hardening takes about thirty minutes to set.

Sometimes plastic pipe is not legal in a given jurisdiction; copper pipe is then the material of choice. There are two kinds of copper pipe: The first is *flexible* copper pipe, and the second is *rigid* copper pipe. The flexible is easier to work with because you can bend it to meet the connection as you can the plastic pipe. The flexible copper pipe has to be supported (if it is a long span) at much more frequent intervals than a *rigid* copper pipe. So if you have a long span, you may want to use the rigid pipe.

Joining Copper Pipe

The two ways of joining copper pipe are threading and soldering. To thread copper pipe, use a threading tool and a flaring tool to make a tight joint. Soldering is a surer way of making watertight connections, but it takes practice. Any plumbing how-to book describes the steps. Replacing or adding plumbing is not a snap, but a recycler *can* learn and by doing so save a considerable amount of money that a plumber would charge.

If you have the older kind of pipe, galvanized iron, and have problems with it, you are better off having a plumber take a look and give an estimate, because the stuff is heavy to handle. Repairing it calls for more know-how.

The only other kind of pipe you will run into is the black cast-iron pipe still used for many drains in the cellar, leading out to the sewer. The pipe, if it leaks at all, will leak when it joins the smaller drain, and that repair is, again, a professional job, unless you want to take lots of time, read up on it, and face it as a challenge. But if you are interested in a quick turn-around, call the plumber.

Your building inspector will tell you what the city plumbing code calls for. In the end whatever you do has to be approved on inspection by him.

Plumbing is pretty much simple logic-plus-experience. There is nothing that complex about it. But, be sure you: (1) want to do it, (2) have the time to do it, and (3) know what the local building code requires before you plunge ahead. And if you do take the plunge, you will find that it's pretty good training in self-reliance.

13

Modern Heating for the Inflationary 1980s

One very promising situation for the recycler is finding a house without central heating. Such a house can be bought cheaply, and installing central heating isn't much work in relation to the amount it will raise the market value of the house.

If an older house *does* have heating, don't fall into the "heating trap," which is to remove the older type of central heating system and install a modern system. Most times, the cost of doing that won't be reflected in the increased sale price of the house. Instead, update the existing heating system. And as we'll see later in the chapter, there are some very good ways of doing just that.

The Fuels and the Carriers

Heat comes in two departments: There's the *fuel* that you use and then there is a *carrier* to distribute the resulting heat throughout the house. Since the carrier (water, steam, etc.) is what you *see* coming into the rooms, heating systems are usually characterized by the carrier rather than the fuel.

The available heating fuels are natural gas, oil, electricity, solar rays, wood, and coal. The available carriers are hot air, steam, hot water, refrigerant, and radiation.

Hot Air Systems

Hot air requires the least expensive installation, regardless of fuel. The system is relatively large, calling for a basement or large crawlspace. Another advantage is that if there's a leak, all that leaks out is hot air. A drawback to a hot air system is that air is less efficient than water as a carrier. Knowledgeable buyers would probably prefer to have a hot water installation, but a hot air installation will not keep a truly interested prospect from buying the house.

Let's look at the fuels for hot air:

Natural gas: A cheaper fuel, in spite of recent price increases. You ought to have a local heating man get figures on this if you are installing a natural gas-hot air system. There might be a saving over oil or electricity of $1000 a year.

Oil: More expensive to install, oil is used where natural gas mains are not available. Once installed oil-hot air is fairly efficient, but the money you save depends on the price of oil at any given time. Ask your local furnace people about that.

Electric: This is the cheapest of all to install, but an electric-hot air system may cost so much to run that you lose out. A buyer may not want to pay the high bills of "all-electric heat."

Solar: Heat can be collected from the sun's rays by installing solar panels on the roof and storing the heat in a water or rock-filled heat reservoir and blowing the heat through the house. But, solar-hot air will be the most expensive system to install by far. Solar is chic and it will help sell the house, but can you sell the house for enough extra money to pay for solar installation?

Passive solar: You *can* set up big windows on the south side of the house and collect sun heat through them, but again, to convert an existing wall to solar windows is very expensive.

Wood: If there is plenty of wood nearby at reasonable prices, a wood-hot air furnace can be competitive with oil and gas systems in installation and fuel cost.

Coal: The new coal-hot air furnaces are self-feeding. Coal is getting cheaper by comparison with other fuels these days. It may be well worth installing.

Hot Water Carrier Systems

Hot water systems are technically more efficient to run than hot air, but cost more to install. Instead of installing the large ducts that carry hot air, you are installing small hot water pipes throughout the house. (If the house already has an installed hot water system, do your best to preserve it.) Hot water systems have a small furnace (one that can be installed on the first floor) and its radiators are relatively small.

Natural gas, as fuel: It is the most economical (at this writing), but the price of gas-hot water may go up as natural gas is decontrolled.

Oil: The most popular, since it is more widely available and, in some places, now competitive with natural gas.

Electric: Very compact, but you pay more to run it.

Solar: Most popular of the solar systems is solar-hot water. The water runs directly from the solar panels through the house without calling for an expensive storage unit. But, you do need a back-up since solar only works when the sun is sufficiently bright. Installation is very expensive. A government incentive program giving tax breaks will help.

Coal: The latest coal-hot water furnaces are care-free. All you have to do is take ashes out once a week. Coal is getting cheaper every year, by comparison with oil and natural gas.

Steam, Refrigerant, and Radiant Carriers

Steam: Older houses generally heat by steam radiators with oil or coal as fuel. Steam pipes tend to leak since they are under pressure. A leak requires expensive repair. Operating costs are greater than with hot water. But, if you deal with an existing steam system there are ways that it can be made more efficient, as we shall see.

Refrigerant: A sort of "antifreeze," or refrigerator-type carrier is used in *heat pumps.*

Stand by the outside screen of any air conditioner: You feel heat coming out, an exhaust product of the cooling process. Now turn that air conditioner around in the window so it cools the outdoors and heats the indoors. You have a heat pump.

Heat pumps use electric fuel. Operation can be very expensive, but if you combine it with central air conditioning it can be economical.

Radiant: Electrically heated radiation panels send out electromagnetic waves that warm any solid object (exactly like the radiant heat of the sun). Since the cost of electrical current is high, radiant heat panels are useful only where it is difficult or expensive to use other installations.

Recycling the Heating System

In a recycle, either (1) you have no central heat and you are free to choose the best system. Or (2) you have an existing system that can be upgraded to an acceptable neighborhood standard. Generally, if there is some sort of central heating, you can figure on being able to make do without spending more than a few hundred dollars.

If there is *no* central heating, get expert help estimating the costs of various options. After that, figure out whether you will be better off spending more money on the heating system and less on insulating, or vice versa, since the two go together.

Choosing a New System

Let's say you have no system presently. The most common choice is to install gas-hot air. If gas is not available, then oil-hot air (or oil-hot water if you need a smaller furnace than a hot air furnace).

Installing a hot air system with ducts is much easier and

cheaper than putting in hot water pipe plus the necessary radiators. If you can combine a hot air carrier with natural gas, you have the most economical system.

Hot water: A hot water system does have one advantage: It can be regulated at any point by installing a temperature valve. For instance, a valve can keep a bedroom at a low temperature while the rest of the house is kept rather warm. The valve can be reset at night to heat the bedroom to a normal temperature.

Heat pump: Practical (as noted) when central air conditioning is included.

Wood: If you have an ample, cheap wood supply, a wood-fired furnace will be competitive with oil or coal.

Solar: Avoid solar unless the neighborhood standard requires it. If you have a very undistinguished house that is a "cleaning woman's special," then you might consider solar as a selling feature. Once solar is installed, it is so inexpensive to operate that any prospective buyer's face will light up when he sees the figures.

Inspecting Existing Systems

The weak point of the hot air system is the heat exchanger, consisting of hollow metal parts up in the stack. The hot gases from fuel combustion rise around the hollow heat exchanger to heat the air *inside* the exchanger. This is the air distributed throughout the house. If there are cracks in the heat exchanger's metal skin, then the host combustion gases from the furnace will seep into the exchanger and be pumped all over the house—unhealthy gases mixing with the air you breathe. So check out the heat exchanger for cracks.

Replacing the heat exchanger is not cheap and will add to your recycling cost estimate.

The hot air furnace ought to create a good draft up the ducts. Remove the upper panel on the furnace and hold a lighted match next to the flue; turn the furnace on. The draft should suck the match flame up the flue. If the draft is weak, add a blower to create a strong one.

The weak point of the hot water system is the cast-iron boiler, good for forty to fifty years. If the house is older than that, you may have a crack in the boiler. A small pool of water at the bottom of the furnace is the telltale sign. The water does no harm but indicates that you may have to replace the boiler. And that costs money. (There are short-term measures, such as adding a compound very much like the product used to stop radiator leaks in cars, but that is not a permanent cure.) If you see puddles, or rust stains (from rusty boiler water) on the hot water furnace or floor nearby, it's time to call a heating engineer.

Upgrading Existing Systems

In each kind of system, there are things you can do to improve the efficiency.

Hot air: Change the filter in the furnace if it is dirty. All hot air furnaces have removable air filters and when they get dirty they impede the flow of air through the ducts, cutting down on the efficiency. Vacuum the blower motor. It works better if free of heavy dust. Check all the hot air registers to make sure they are open and clean.

If your furnace does not have a blower, or if one of the ducts isn't warming the room, add one or more blowers outside the furnace. Cut into the ducts and install the blower and thermostat. This is a top-of-the-ladder job. Make sure you have *time* to do this kind of thing before you commit to recycling the house.

Above all, on your first recycle, call in a furnace maintenance man and go over the heat system with him (preferably before you have bought the house). You can save yourself lots of time and energy by listening to what the expert says. (Of course not all experts are expert, but that is a chance you take. Try to get one with good references.)

Upgrading the Hot Water System

Older hot water systems are often clogged with pipe scale. Reduce it by using a chemical that dissolves scale.

If your current heating system relies on convection to circulate water to the radiators, consider adding a circulating pump to the return pipe. The water, moving faster through the system, has less time to cool off, and saves on fuel.

Steam systems: Replace the old radiator valves with new ones so that they let air out more effectively. The radiator should be full of hot steam rather than have it half-full of stagnant air. Replace whole radiators with a newer finned pipe radiator, which is more efficient, but don't mix the two. The finned pipe cools faster and will not heat a room in the same cycle as the cast-iron radiator.

Radiant heat: Adding radiant heat panels to warm any single room, is usually cheaper than adding ducts or hot water pipe. Radiant heat costs more to run but, if used only occasionally, it will not add much to the heating bill.

In recycling the heating system, your main weapons are (1) your pencil for figuring costs of the various options, and (2) expert advice for situations where experience can help avoid pitfalls, as well as calculate the effect of local conditions.

The decisions you make about your heating system have to be well-informed. Spend time accumulating information. The substantial cost of changes has to be justified by an even more substantial increase in the market value of the house.

14

Modern Electrical Service for the Profitable Recycle

The modernizing of the electrical system in a house can be one of the best sources of profit. If you find a house lacking, for instance, automatic laundry and dishwasher installations because the house electrical service doesn't have the capacity to carry the required current, then you have a gold mine. Nothing pushes the price of a house down more than an old fashioned laundry and kitchen. No family wants to live there. Yet to install them means to install a new "electrical service." And that is just what the recycler does.

The state of the house's electrical system can easily be ascertained by inspecting the "service panel" that contains the fuses or breaker switches that protect all the house's circuits. All the house electricity comes in on one side of the service panel and leaves from the other side—for various parts of the house. It's Grand Central Station for the electricity of the house.

If the panel is, say thirty to fifty years old, it will contain fuses rather than breaker switches and only eight or ten of those. This means the whole house has only eight or ten circuits total, probably representing a *capacity* of 40 to 60 amps of current. certainly not enough to carry the amperage required by modern electrical appliances. Today's modern service panel carries 150 amps or so.

To increase capacity, people sometimes screw in 30 amp fuses for circuits originally designed for a 15 amp or 20 amp capacity. The wires are carrying more electricity than they were designed for. That is dangerous. They can overheat and even start fires. You need to put in more capacity.

Estimating the Electrical Costs

Where the electrical system is inadequate you can be talking about a $1000 cost for recycling it if you hire an electrician. But that $1000 is well spent because the house becomes much more marketable at a much higher price.

Call an electrician and get his estimate for rewiring; add his estimate to your costs of recycling, and lower your bid accordingly. (An experienced recycler can estimate closely what it is going to cost him in time or money to put in a new service. That skill takes experience with different houses; some houses rewire easily, others with difficulty. If you are inexperienced, let an electrician do the estimate.)

A Modern Electrical Service

The modern three-wire system comes with one "neutral wire" wrapped in white and with two "hot wires" usually wrapped in red and in black. Each hot wire carries "phased 120 volt current." Either hot wire will drive electricity at 120 volts of force through an appliance into the "neutral wire." But, if a washer-drier or dishwasher requires 240 volts, you connect the appliance between the two "hot wires," to give you a 240 volt drive through the appliance. This option of doubling the voltage is one feature that makes the modern electrical service panel worth installing.

The modern service panel has another advantage: circuit

breakers, which trip, rather than fuses, which blow, when too much current runs through. An overload on a circuit trips the breaker, and when you find the cause of the overload and remove it, you can flip the breaker back into position. The breaker will flip right out again if the circuit is still overloaded. This gives you another chance to find the problem. [The old-fashioned fuses burned out and you had to screw in a new one. If you had a recurrent problem (short-circuit) on one circuit, you could run out of fuses while trying to find it.]

Putting in a New Service

If you have time and want the experience and your local building codes allow it, you (under the supervision of an electrician who comes in to approve your work) can put in a new service yourself. To start, you have the electric utility company run a bigger line to the house. They also will install a new meter. The suspension cable that carries an electrical cable is fastened to the service head. From there the electrical cable is run into the new service panel, which you have installed.

Before you order a new service panel, make an "electrical diagram" of the house so that you know exactly how many of what kind of circuit breakers you want in the panel. (You may need the help of an electrician, unless you have done it before.) Locate on a floor plan all appliances, down to the last light. Then figure out how many of what capacity are to go on one circuit.

You run separate 240 volt circuits to your washer-drier, dishwasher, and electric hot water heater. You run separate 120 volt lines to those appliances that are liable to trip a circuit breaker: toaster, curling iron, hair drier, blenders, shop tools. All are typically liable to trip circuit breakers. (You don't want to have your lights go out just because they're on the same line with such an appliance.)

Finishing Out Your Diagram

Appliances such as electric lights which are not normally going to trip a circuit breaker can be put one, two, three, or four to a circuit. This will cut down on the complexity of the wiring. Be sure to have at least one light in each room on a different circuit than all the other lights. If one line does go out, you still have one light in the room.

Use 15 amp circuit breakers for the lines with only a few appliances that have a light load. If one appliance "shorts out," the circuit breaker trips quickly. For lines with a heavier load, use a 20 amp circuit breaker. The idea is that the circuit breaker should trip quickly whenever an appliance malfunctions to avoid heating up the wires inside the walls at the risk of electrical fire.

Safety in Electrical Systems

There are two kinds of safety involved in electrical work. The first is the safety of the person doing the electrical work. The second is the safety of those using the appliances.

To do any electrical work, first shut off the circuit. Do not simply turn off the local switch, but go back to the service panel and pull the circuit breaker. The wires in the switch box can reconnect if you are working on the wiring.

Make sure there is no current in the line or appliance. Use a "circuit tester" which lights up if the line is "live." Circuit testers cost very little and can save you a lot of grief. An electrical shock, even a mild one, is unpredictable in its results. It can interfere with heart rhythm. Don't be casual about working on electrical circuits.

The Nature of the Electrical Accident

All electrical accidents start with a short circuit. A short circuit isn't literally a *short* path, but is a circuit created accidentally which is so wide open that current surges through heavily, heating up the wires and appliance during its surge.

Let's take a toaster, for example; the current goes in one side, heats up the elements of the toaster, and goes out the other side, having done its work. But it has traveled a hard-working path, through the resistance of the toaster. *Now* if you stick your fingers into the toaster or stick a metal fork inside while the toaster is operating, the electricity may find an easier path (short circuit) up your fingers and down through your legs to the floor, giving you a jolt. For a second there, you become part of the short circuit, an easier path for electricity than the hard path through the toaster. The reason it flows easily through you is that your body contains so much water. Anything wet represents a very easy path, just as does anything metal.

Shoes will usually save you from a serious shock; they are made of dry, fibrous material that is hard for much electricity to travel through. Any such material is called "electrical insulation." But, remove that insulation from your feet and go barefoot; immediately electricity travels more easily through your body. If your feet are wet, your body becomes a much easier path: Electricity will surge violently and you receive a very big shock. Never handle electrical appliances (including power tools) if your feet are wet; it is too risky.

The Use of the "House Ground"

Appliances can "burn out" (have an internal short circuit). Then, the hot wire inside the appliance may connect to the case of the appliance: Let's say that you have dry shoes on. Instead of going through you, the electricity finds an easier path through the "house ground" wire, a "fourth wire" in every modern appliance cable. It is connected to the case of the appliance. This wire, if you peel back the end of an electrical cord sold today, is a bright, bare or paper-wrapped wire. (The other three wires have rubberlike insulation wrapped around them.) The function of the fourth "house ground" wire is to draw off stray electricity. The house ground wire provides an easy path for straying electricity short-circuited to the appliance case. The path leads back down to the outlet in the wall and from there to the outside of the house and finally to a metal stake driven deep into the moist ground. (It is called a "ground wire" because it takes errant electricity back to the ground outside.)

Let's say an appliance burns out and is not connected

properly to the house ground. Then, the electricity uses *you* as the short circuit from the case back to ground, and you get a jolt before the circuit breaker trips.

Nothing like that happens if the appliance is grounded properly. The instant that the electricity connects to the appliance case, the electricity surges through the house ground wire—before anyone touches the case—and your circuit breaker trips. So you had a problem, but you didn't have to get a shock to find it out.

You cannot, however, assume the ground wire system will always protect you. The house ground wire can disconnect and you can still become the short circuit. Make sure your shoes are dry, that you are not standing in a damp place, nor touching any "natural ground" like gas or plumbing pipes. If the floor where you are working is damp, put down a piece of dry scrap plywood to stand on.

Installing a New Circuit

Assume that you decide to add a circuit to a room. You want to put up ceiling lights, let's say. There are two options: (1) Lead the wire in from an unused circuit breaker in the service panel, or (2) add on to the existing circuit, if it has sufficient capacity to carry the extra current.

Capacity, or flow of electricity, is always rated in *amps*. (The *drive* or force that it has is rated in *volts*). Do not put more amps through a circuit than its wire is designed for. Every light bulb draws some amps and so does every appliance. You add all the amps of appliances on the circuit to find out how many amps now flow in the circuit.

Let's say you have five 50-watt lights on a line. Since watts = amps x volts, in a 120-volt circuit, you have five amps drawing about one-half amp each or 2½ amps total for the circuit. You can easily add more amps without overloading, if the circuit breaker or fuse is rated at 15 amps.

The wiring for the new circuit can go either inside the walls or on the walls. Some codes allow you to use on-the-wall conduits or "surface wire." You can buy decorative-looking conduits that are much safer than stringing extension cords around, and much less work than breaking into the walls or ceiling to run the wires behind the walls.

But let us say that you have decided to run the wires inside the walls: Enter the walls from below in the basement or from the ceiling, depending on where it's easier to connect to the nearest supply of electricity. (If you already have outlets in the room, go directly from an outlet.)

To go up from the basement to wire a ceiling light, you break into the wall at floor level, drill down inside the wall to the basement. Then thread the wire up from the basement through the hole. Next, you cut a hole at the junction of wall and ceiling, drop a line down and fish up the cable from the floor hole with a semirigid "fish tape." Now, cut a hole in the ceiling for the overhead light. Push the fish tape from that hole toward the hole at the edge of the ceiling, snag the cable, and pull the cable back to the ceiling hole. You're wired.

Variations on this system will enable you to add outlets, lamps, switches, and fixtures wherever you need them in a room, but it takes time. It also takes some homework. There are whole books on rewiring houses. Before you actually tackle such a job (in preference to having an electrician do it), read up on the subject.

Intelligent Recycling Electrically

Adding a new service or at least a dozen new circuits is a top-of-the-ladder kind of job. Don't undertake too many such jobs in a given house. And be sure your bid reflects the cost of top-of-the-ladder renovations. Too many top-of-the-ladder jobs make a house too expensive a recycle. On your first recycle don't take on more than one top-of-the-ladder job yourself. A complete wiring of the whole house would take several months of spare time—nights and weekends.

Now we have finished a survey of recycling the systems—insulation, plumbing, heating, and electrical. This concludes Step 7 of recycling and we can go on to Step 8, the exteriors and interiors.

part V

Giving Your Recycle Maximum Selling Power

15

Exteriors to Bring Prospects in Off the Street

We begin with exteriors, the first part of Step 8 of recycling. The exterior is the house's best pitch. If the potential buyer falls in love with it, he is half sold. After all, the exterior represents the owner to the world. An attractive exterior will bring prospects in off the street. In real estate, this is known as "curb appeal."

Inspecting the Roof

Looking from the outside: When a shingle roof is ready to give up the ghost, most of the shingles are curled at the lip, and some are missing. Asphalt shingles last about 20 years. If you think they need replacing, call a roofing man or contractor to see what it would cost.

If you have cedar-shake shingle and the shingles are worn to a nub of their former selves, the same advice applies.

Looking under the eaves: You can confirm your ideas about the roof by looking at the attic ceiling. Leaks will show up in discolored and rotted ceiling boards and rafters.

A rotting roof can require rebuilding the entire roof. Only if the poor shape of the roof is reflected in a correspondingly low asking price do you have a good recycle situation.

Some Hints About Looking

If you look at the very edge of a roof, you can see whether or not the house has "a second roof," (a second layer of felt laid on over the first). If the house needs a third roof, everything has to be torn off because a house can only support "two roofs," maximum.

Also look at the ridge line. Hold a ruler or straight-edge up to it and you will see, even from the ground, whether or not the ridge sags. If it does, it may mean the house has not settled evenly, and there may be a big engineering problem here. Or a sagging ridge may mean that the rafters have rotted and sagged.

Take a look at the flashing, the metal pieces around the chimneys and vents. If the flashing seems bent or rusty and cracked, you may have to replace it. It's probably leaking right now.

If there is a chimney, has it pulled slightly away from the house? If so, that can mean the chimney footing has settled poorly. Again, a contractor or civil engineer should have a look.

In the attic, light spotty discoloring in the rafters or beams may mean dry rot has set in, caused by lack of ventilation. If limited in extent, any rot can be repaired. If dry rot has really taken hold of the rafters, you have to replace them—big job.

Take a look at the house exterior walls. You can utilize the horizontal lines of clapboard siding to see if the house has foundation problems. Sight down along the lines. If there is a downward dip at the far corner, it may mean that corner has settled further than the others and you have a cracked foundation or potential for one. Again, a civil engineer should be called in to check.

If you have brick or stucco walls, look along the walls to see if you can spot any bulging sections. A bulge is a sign of serious ongoing structural failure. There may be good reason to avoid buying that house unless you have an estimate for the repair and the seller's willingness to accept a low enough bid to take into account the cost of repair.

If the siding or shingling or stucco is only deteriorated (not bulging or dipping), the repairs are not that complex. An exterior that is shabby can often be brightened quickly by repainting or by installing new siding.

Payoff Exterior Jobs

The most delightful payoff in recycling is painting the house. It's a low-cost high-reward job. Scrape the old paint down, fill the cracks with caulk, and apply new paint. The cost of labor, plus the cost of new paint (which can vary from $300 for a small house to $1500 for a mansion), can raise the market value of the house by 10 percent.

After painting, the next most profitable recycle work is restoring the trim and patching the siding.

To restore the trim: Match missing pieces at the lumber yard. Or the previous owner may have picked up fallen pieces of trim and stored them in or around the house. (Never throw away any old painted boards found on the grounds or in the basement.)

To patch the siding: Cut out rotted pieces of siding with an electric saber saw. Slide closely-cut new pieces in and prime with a coat of paint. Fill any cracks in siding with caulk. Give it a final coat. You can hardly see the repair.

To restore the roof: Put planks down to spread your weight on the roof to avoid causing more damage. Repair cracked and torn shingles by coating under them with roof tar or putting a piece of metal flashing underneath. Replace all the cracked, rusty, bent flashing in the valleys and around a chimney or a vent. Go over leaky sections with a tar brush and a gallon bucket of roofing tar. (If that works, you are saved the more expensive job of reroofing.) Restore its good looks by spray painting the whole roof with a water-based paint. This evens out the spotty look of the tar patches. But now suppose there are lots of leaky sections. That means reroofing. You can't save a roof that far gone.

Reroofing the House

The reroofing of a house involves putting on a new roofing felt and shingles over the old roof. If your house already has a second roof, then you tear off both layers of shingle and the underlying roofing felt and start over again laying felt and shingles. You may consider hiring professionals; reroofing often is surprisingly reasonable. Pros can do it fast, and you will be a long time reroofing, unless you've done it before.

The most common shingles are asphalt, and the next most common are cedar shake. The cedar shake roof is definitely more expensive, five times the cost of an asphalt roof to replace.

Some kinds of roof, such as slate shingles or tile, are very expensive pro jobs. Never bid on a house where such a roof needs replacement, unless the cost of repair is reflected in the bid.

Restoring the sides and restoring the roof actually account for more than half the ordinary recycle exterior repairs. The other half includes cutting away and replacing rotting cornices and rafter ends, and putting aluminum sheet over ruined window sills. There are many reference books that will help you cope with such projects, setting them out step by step. A friendly local hardware store will advise. Have a carpenter come over and look over the problems.

Redesigning the Exterior

The recycler looks for simple and inexpensive ways to improve the outside look of the house by adding visually exciting and appealing features. The simplest and least expensive way is to add trim where there is none. A simple two-board corner trim dresses up a house immensely.

There are various other kinds of trim you can put in: window trim, shutters, door trim, etc. My favorite is window boxes.

These are, to some degree, more expensive and time-consuming than corner trim, but may well be worth the effort. You can get inspiration from the building supply catalogs, decorator magazines, and just by riding around well-kept neighborhoods. You see one house that is well-trimmed and decorated; beside it, another house with the same construction but without trim looks dowdy and dull.

When replacing siding that is worn, faded, or out of date, it is absolutely necessary to use something like cedar plywood or board siding to create a house that has a very up-to-date look. (Let's assume now that the neighborhood has many houses already with a modern look.) Siding is expensive but there are recycles where simple repainting will not be sufficient.

There is a very inexpensive siding: rough-sawn board exteriors, put on vertically or on the diagonal. It makes the house look appealingly casual and family-oriented. Other choices for new siding are many. Every building supply outlet has a yard full. Ask them what's selling and why.

Letting in Light

Modern houses are built to let in light. One of the most elegant ways to renovate is to replace a wood door with sliding glass. Open your recycle up to a view via a sliding glass door and outside deck, and turn a stodgy undistinguished house into a breathtaking contemporary one. (Assuming now that the house isn't a gloriously traditional one in a traditional neighborhood.) That kind of thing is precisely what you are looking for: a rather dramatic change for relatively little time and money.

Not every house adapts to it, but a house otherwise undistinguished will stand out by adding a picture window in a strategic location—southern exposure. Cost is reasonable and it will warm up the house on cold days, at no added expense.

Adding Separate Construction

If the house you are recycling has considerable grounds and no outbuilding other than a garage, adding a small, simple garden shed will create visual excitement. An outbuilding will not raise the asking price, but it is a strong selling point.

Add a free-form garden pool to serve as a center or focus of an otherwise uninteresting space behind the house. Or, you can add an "open roof" structure for vines to grow on; or, make a post-and-beam roof for an outdoor table and barbecue grill. These are the touches that sell houses, but make sure you are not spending so much on an effect that you lose your profit.

And Finally Landscaping It

It is extremely important to landscape properly for curb appeal. You need to seed a new lawn in time to have it grow in by the time the rest of the recycle is finished. You may need a couple of months' head start on landscape effects.

Where you have a steeply pitched lawn, you might consider a retaining wall to give a split-level lawn look. Stone steps lead from the level of the upper lawn to the lower lawn—a very nice way to dress up a piece of property.

Now, when it comes to hedges, trees, and such, you can have them hauled in and planted full size, zap! like that. But this is expensive. You are more likely to want to purchase some modest plantings, to move an existing hedge to a more appropriate spot, or to add a few modest bushes and shrubs near the foundation to complement the house.

16

Recycling Interiors to Create Fabulous Bargains

The second part of Step 8 of recycling is to create new interiors. Take a house with unserviceable, outmoded or poor design and with damaged or dirty ceilings, walls, and floors and make it a modern, convenient, sparklingly refinished interior. It is typically an interior transformation that makes any recycle a good buy. Most houses built more than a decade ago cannot now be duplicated new for the recycle price. Thus, this house, recycled with a renovated interior is *very* desirable.

Even so, the interior has to take a back seat in the budget to the house systems and exterior. No one is going to buy a house with a malfunctioning electrical system, faulty plumbing, poor insulation, or shabby exterior. Only when you pick a recycle where the systems and the exterior are in good shape, can you use most of the money you have budgeted for upgrading the interior. But, when you *can* focus on the interior design and renovation, you then make a recycle a fabulous bargain, truly.

Interior Design of Space

Creative design of interior space comes first; then you renovate the ceilings, walls, and floors. Unless the original house had an architect, the recycler can usually improve on its use of space. Many older houses were designed for large families. There was no provision for modern electrical appliances (dishwasher, etc.). Some of the newer houses that have been allowed to deteriorate were designed to be built inexpensively, not to provide a good family and social life.

Let's look at three terms that make clear the function of good design.

Private space: where the family is to be safe from intrusion by outsiders, including bedroom and adjoining bath, study, sewing room, family room, and the like.

Public space: where family and visitors socialize and dine, including dining room, kitchen, living room, fireplace room, nonadjoining bathrooms.

Traffic space: connects public to private space and both to the outdoors—includes entrances, porchways, foyers, halls, back porch, and corridors.

Good design lets each of these serve their purposes without undue intrusion from the other. For example, you don't set a study so that it has to serve to connect two other rooms. You don't connect two bedrooms unless one is a nursery. You separate the kids' play space from the living room, so as to have a place where adults can socialize free of toys underfoot. That's one set of ideas.

A single generalization is that modern design creates more open space than old-fashioned design. Today, people like large rooms. They like a kitchen separated only by a counter from the dining room. You can have traffic space at one end of a living room; you don't need a hallway.

Making Space in an Old House

You can start out by using the same floor plan you drew up in order to get your recycle estimate (See Chapter 7). In my experience, this floor plan changes somewhat as you work on the house and get more familiar with it. That is fine as long as the changes don't add significant cost.

The goal of changes in an older house is to make the right-size spaces—not too large for intimacy and not too small for comfort. The recycle interior plan section in the middle of Chapter 7 examines the ways in which you can make space the right size and find "new space" that was hidden away before. Once you've made your plan connect all the doorways with arrows, one to the other, and see if your traffic space relates your public space and private space in the most effective manner. If you can create shorter arrows, then do so.

Now, we've got our design.

Let's go on to renovate.

Renovate Ceilings First

Do your ceilings first and then the walls and then the floor. Then, the debris and paint spilling down from the ceiling can be cleaned up when you do the walls, and the debris from the wall can be cleaned up when you do the floor.

Ceilings are made of either sheetrock or plaster, unless it is a very unusual house. If these are discolored, flaked, scarred, or uneven, they have to be worked on before you paint. Heavy discoloring is going to need a coat of sizing paint first. Scars or uneven spots will show up if you plan to paint in a light color to make the room seem as large as possible. (That is why almost all rooms are painted in light colors.) A lump seems like a mound; a scratch is a deep scar. So scrape off the old paint and then sand off any lumps. Fill dents or cuts with plaster or spackle. If you have large holes, use Structuralite or some other heavier filler. If the ceiling is really bad though, it pays to simply cover with sheetrock rather than spend days filling and sanding.

You can put up a stucco or tile ceiling. These cost more than sheetrock, but may be more appropriate to the house you are recycling. Or, you can wallpaper the ceilings. But, of course, it takes more hands to hold wallpaper in place on the ceiling until it sticks than it does when you wallpaper the walls.

(Today, almost no one replasters ceilings unless doing an authentic restoration. Plastering is a rare and expensive skill in this age of easily installed sheetrock or wall tile.)

You may have ceiling moldings that are damaged. If you do, find someone to restore the molding or learn to do it yourself. There are few artisans today who can copy moldings. There are how-to books that tell you how to copy moldings—a real challenge. The alternative is to buy all new moldings.

If it is a dull-looking room, you can liven it by using a texture paint on the ceiling. This paint goes on in thick swirls to give a stucco-like appearance without all the trouble of actual stucco.

In a one-story house, you can give the rooms a more spacious feeling at very little expense by removing the flat ceiling and putting sheet rock over the inside roof to create the "cathedral ceiling."

Doing Interior Walls

As with ceilings, walls are generally sheetrock or plaster. If I spend money anywhere in the interior renovation, it is in wallpapering rather than painting the walls. Wallpaper is much more expensive than paint, but fairly easy to do (as compared to wallpapering ceilings). Wallpaper gives so much more to a room than a simple off-white coat of paint. If there is money in the recycle budget, I go even further and use vinyl wallpaper. Vinyl is four times as expensive as ordinary wallpaper, but families love it because you can just wipe it clean with a soapy rag. If a child throws jam against the wall, you don't have to repaint, just wash.

When painting the walls (as in the ceiling), if there is substantial discoloring you are going to have to put on a sizing coat after you scrape off the flaked old paint, sand, and fill to make a smooth surface. In a recycle with a rather limited budget, painting is the wall finish of choice.

Whenever you paint over old wallpaper you need a primer

coat. But if the old wallpaper is not smooth you have to steam it off. If the old walls are really in poor shape, simply sheetrock over them and start afresh.

Texture paints give a wonderful look to walls of an otherwise mundane room. Another option is inexpensive cork wall tile.

The most expensive kind of renovation is putting up wood paneling. If you have a house that is nothing special, you can make it special by putting cedar paneling in one room. If you want the house to sell quickly because the interest meter is running, you may need that "special room." Every house has to have at least one special feature as a selling point to distinguish it from others of like price.

Watch out for the "decorator trap" though. Don't start paneling several rooms (unless all the other houses in the neighborhood have paneling in more than one room).

Renovating the Floors

You have one happy resource in renovating floors: carpeting. It is less expensive to carpet than to sand and refinish a floor that is cracked and discolored. Not only is carpeting less expensive, but it adds a warmth to the room that hardwood floor cannot. A bedroom with a hardwood floor looks cold and *feels* cold. A carpet is more inviting.

All wall-to-wall carpeting ought to be done by professionals: They do it so cheaply that it is not worth learning the art of carpeting and doing it yourself. Plus, you have to rent the stretching devices to insure the carpet stays smooth and flat while being installed.

Carpeting makes such a magnificent splash that it is worth the money even if the floors in the bedrooms are in OK shape. This is particularly true if you keep a sharp eye out for carpet sales, and go early in the morning to get the best buys.

In public space nothing makes a statement as strong as a beautifully refinished hardwood floor with a few area rugs for contrast. Here it does not matter that the wood is gleaming and cold. *People* warm up a public space.

Inexpensive linoleums are fine for kitchen and bathroom floors, and they are easy to install. I have installed many linoleum floors myself. You cut it to shape and glue it down from the middle outward. The job takes time but is relatively amateur-proof.

Floor tiles cost much more and make a much stronger statement. Professionals should install tile. Unless installed exactly so, tiles will come loose in the hard use given kitchen and bathroom floors. One of my biggest recycling failures came when I installed a tile kitchen floor and had to have professionals come in and replace it several months later.

Color Schemes for Recycling

Thousands of decorating books have been written around color schemes: They are full of good ideas, some especially pertinent to recycling.

Pick a color scheme for the house. Carry it through the house so that the house "has continuity." Making every room "individual" can create a jumbled feeling to the house. If you want to create the feeling of spaciousness, use light colors. If you want to create a smaller, more intimate feeling, as in a bedroom, you can use darker colors.

If you have a ranch or Spanish style house, you can go with darker, more earthy tones. The contemporary designs are better served by lighter colors, from monochromatic white to beige, set off by darker more earthy colors, and by textured wall fabrics.

If you have a small room, it has to be painted in light colors or it will seem to close in on the occupants. Light colors "push a wall back' while darker ones bring a wall in. You can make a long narrow room seem in better proportion by having the end walls slightly darker. A high ceiling can be "brought down" by a darker color.

If you have a window with a good view or handsome wood moldings, paint it a different color to contrast with the rest.

In "open-house plans" where one room merges into the next, "marry" each room to those next to it by reversing the color scheme as you procede from one to the next.

Making Lines Make Space

A low-ceilinged room can be made to seem more spacious by emphasizing all the vertical lines in the room. Contrasting strips of wood between cabinets is one way. Vertically striped wallpaper is another.

Narrow rooms can be "widened" in the same way—by horizontal lines.

Using Paints to Good Effect

"Texture paints" and "sand paints" give a feeling of informality to a room; slick, smooth paints give a more formal feeling.

Flat paints should be used in different instances than semigloss. Use a flat latex paint for interiors where there's little need for regular washing and scrubbing: living rooms, dining rooms, bedrooms, and ceilings. The flat paints cover well, and go on easily.

Switch to flat alkyd and oil-based paints for wood, wallboard and metal surfaces; these hang on better and are more damage proof. They can be put on thicker and wash better.

Semigloss paints are good to use in kitchens, bathrooms, laundries, and wherever you will regularly wash down the walls and ceilings. The semigloss will stand repeated scrubbings without wearing thin.

Finishing Coat for Wood

It's better to use a penetrating oil rather than varnish to finish off wood trim, since varnish scratches. But if you do have varnish, a good paste wax coat will give it protection against scratching.

The most durable shiny finishes for wood, if that is what you want, are epoxy and polyurethane. They are extremely tough.

Making Wallcoverings work

Wallcoverings, such as wallpaper, vinyl wallpaper, textured cloth, wood, etc., can be applied to make rooms smaller or larger, and they "change" the proportions, using the same principles noted for paint and use of lines. For instance, a small room will need a light pattern wallcovering to make it spacious, whereas a large room will be cozier with wallcovering that has a darker, more dense pattern.

(Check your walls, though, to see if they are perfectly square to each other and to the ceilings and floors. If they are at slight angles, then above all else, avoid wallcoverings with definite stripes or square patterns.)

If you have walls that are dented and uneven—even after preparation—a rough texture wallcovering or one with embossed design will partly cancel the unevenness.

Wallcovering and draperies can be bought so as to coordinate in feeling, so that the room seems to be smooth, all of a piece. If you have contrasting wallcoverings and drapes, you break the room into different odd shapes. To keep the same smooth look, paint the woodwork the same or complementary color as the wallcovering.

You can also cover walls with decorative wood paneling or boards: knotty pine, redwood, chestnut, etc. You can buy boards four to eight inches wide. To accent a wall, use random-width boards. To give a wall a subdued feeling, use boards the same width.

Tiles

Ceramic tiles can give a fine feeling of design and solidity to a wall. Before you decide to use just paint and wallpaper, investigate the possiblity of using tiles: Besides ceramic, there are cork, metal, and plastic tile. Some tiles simulate stone and brick—in special situations these can make a room come alive.

Mirrors

Mirrors can make magic. They can "expand space," or camoflage structural flaws. If you have a room that is too narrow, then mirrors on the side walls will expand the room in that direction. If your room is low ceilinged, then a mirror right at the ceiling line will "raise the roof."

In addition to the regular plain mirror, you can get tinted mirrors whose gray or bronze hues do not distort color values, but give a handsome muted effect while reflecting a room's decor.

Making a Bathroom Glorious

So many bathrooms look as if they'd been taken out of a service station: Use colors, fabrics, and accessories generously to give the bathroom a lively, welcoming feeling. Put in countertops around the sinks and the tub. Set up some plants on these, and hang plants from the walls or ceiling. A bathroom is to live in; an "alive bathroom" is a very persuasive kind of selling point for both men and women.

Review: The Nine Steps of Recycling

1. Finding a house with the right needs in the right neighborhood.
2. Spotting Sure-Fire combinations and bidding low.
3. Getting an advantageous mortgage and other financing.
4. Closing on the purchase legally and conclusively.
5. Making a detailed recycling plan to control costs.
6. Blazing a paper trail to ensure nonstop recycling.
7. Recycling the house systems (plumbing, heating, etc.).
8. Recycling the exterior, interior, and landscaping.
9. Using selling know-how to get a profitable seller.

17

Finding a Mortgage for Your Full-Price Buyer

The final step of recycling is Step 9: selling the house.

You know your house will attract buyers because your house is a "best buy." The critical question is, In this day of scarce mortgages, how can you help the buyer get his mortgage?

There are two main routes: (1) List the house with real estate agents; then, the agents will take part of the responsibility for finding a mortgage. (2) Sell the house yourself: You will save $3000 on a house that sells for $45,000 (and more for houses selling higher).

If you are willing to take time to research the mortgage sources and to qualify the buyer who shows up with serious intent, you can make a substantially bigger profit selling it yourself. In the lower range of house prices ($40,000 to $60,000), it is well worth doing it yourself at least for a month or two. In the midrange, between $60,000 and $90,000, it is a toss-up. From $100,000 and up, you do best to list your house with brokers: People buying in that range go to brokers first, not the

"Houses for Sale" section of the newspaper. Many such buyers are executives on the move: They have contacted real estate agents in advance who will show them houses.

Sources of Mortgage Information

These professionals can help you find mortgage sources for your buyer:

Real estate lawyers
Bank loan officers
Real estate brokers
Mortgage brokers

You must engage a real estate lawyer in the process of selling the house (to represent you at the closing and to draw the contract of sale, etc.), so you may as well take advantage of his knowledge of the mortgage market.

Real estate brokers *have* to know where to get mortgages or they are out of business. Get them to talk to you informally.

Bank loan officers are always available for talks.

Mortgage brokers, specialists whose business it is to find mortgages, stay on top of the mortgage situation daily. They charge a fee to the buyer or to you.

Three Kinds of Mortgages

The three most common kinds of mortgages are:
1. government-sponsored mortgages
2. take-back or owner-financed mortgages
3. "creative" bank mortgages

Government mortgages are attractive in many ways. Many house sales today involve some federal mortgage program: the FHA, Veterans Administration, or other special programs. The present administration in Washington is cutting back on some government-sponsored mortgages, but they are still very important.

For the recycler, qualifying for a particular federal mortgage program takes a good bit of time. You have to submit an application and the house has to be inspected by the government to make sure it meets program standards. The buyer also has to pass inspection.

The usual government program works by insuring a mortgaging bank against default by the buyer (which is no small task). It gives the bank incentive to put up with the inconvenience of the bureaucratic red tape and to charge a lower interest rate. So, even though it is a government program, the actual mortgaging is usually done through a bank.

Government programs specify a top interest rate the bank can charge the buyer; the bank then takes some money out of the seller's (your) hide in *points,* to make up the difference between maximum allowable interest under the program and the going interest rate.

A point is "1 percent" of the selling price payable up front. If the house sells for $50,000 and the bank is charging five points, that means the seller (you) will be paying $2500 to the bank. This comes out of your profit.

The Take-Back (Owner) Mortgage

The recycler selling a house may find that the mortgage market is so tight that he has "to take back some paper." The recycler then becomes the "bank" for some or all of the mortgage, getting the money a little at a time, rather than all at once. A mortgage agreement is complex, nothing that a recycler can write out himself. Only a lawyer can draw up the papers in a bulletproof legal manner.

The take-back can be in the form of a first or second mortgage. If your buyer can get a first mortgage but can't come up with the cash for a down payment, then the recycler (you) can take a private second mortgage for the down payment to put the deal over the top.

Today the first mortgage that you take back ought to

have a variable interest rate so you don't lose out if interest rates rise. You can also protect yourself the way the banks do by getting a "balloon" every few years. A "balloon" means you renegotiate the whole mortgage periodically at current market

Your lawyer's work should give you: (1) the highest possible interest rate, (2) a solid down payment, (3) a thorough credit check to qualify the buyer (here the realty agent can help, if there is one). It is possible to get an additional agreement from the buyer to be personally responsible for the mortgage, in case you repossess and the sale of the house does not cover the remaining mortgage. (You can get it out of the buyer's salary or bank account.)

A final word: A take-back mortage is a last resort. If you take back a mortgage and then need the cash, your only recourse is to sell the mortgage. And any mortgage-buyer will pay considerably less than the face value of the mortgage.

The Creative Bank Mortgage

The "creative bank mortgage" is very different from the traditional mortgage, but creative mortgages are *available* today while traditional bank mortgages are not. Banks will often give mortgages only if it either "balloons" every five years or its interest rate varies with the commercial interest rate. Bank policies are changing. This is an era of experimentation varying from state to state—even from city to city. So find out just what the situation is.

To sum up mortgages: Sellers *are* finding mortgage money today for prospective buyers, and so are real estate agents. Houses are being sold all the time, changing hands as houses always have. The recycler has only to find out how he can help his buyer put together the financing.

Qualifying the Buyer

Let's say you have agreed with the buyer on the price. The next step is finding out if he *can* qualify for a mortgage. In other words, you have to "qualify the buyer." You need to know: (1) the prospect's salary, (2) what liquid funds he has, (3) his position in his company and how long he has worked there, (4) his bank connections, and (5) the result of a standard credit check through a credit agency—they do it for a fee.

18

Intelligent Selling to Maximize the Recycle Profit

We come to the completion of Step 9: presenting and selling the house you have recycled. Selling for the highest price requires the following:

1. Solid preparation prior to showing
2. Convincing presentation during showing
3. Immediate signing of contracts
4. Interim follow-up maintenance
5. Completed formal closing

Let's start with preparation:

Preparing a house for showing is like putting on a play: Don't rely on the buyer's imagination to fill the gaps. Most people cannot visualize a finished product when faced with an empty space.

Don't succumb to the temptation to show the house empty or partially complete. This will turn the buyer off even if the buyer is not aware of it. Not only should all the carpentry be complete but the interior should have at least minimal furnishing: kitchen complete with appliances, curtains, rugs, and some inexpensive furniture in all rooms.

The outside of the house must be finished: siding painted, lawns in place.

Presentation of the House

There are two faces of presentation: first, there is advertising—presenting at a distance; then there is the face-to-face presentation—showing the house.

The trick to advertising a house, either by listing with realty agents or advertising in local papers, is to get a maximum number of people intrigued enough to look at the house. There is a whole language of advertising, a way of "writing copy" that you must become familiar with to write successful ads.

The best way to learn this "new language" is to go over the local newspaper classified real estate section with a broker. He can tell you what all the little abbreviations mean and what the "code words" stand for. (The kitchen and laundry appliances, for instance, are important; so are the number of bedrooms and baths and the size of the lot.) After you go through several real estate sections armed with input from a broker, you will be able to compose a good ad. Sometimes you can be creative to good advantage. I once ran a standard ad for a house, got very little response, and then rewrote the ad to say, "Cutest little house you ever saw." The response was instant and tremendous. The house sold in two days.

The best placement for classified ads is in the Sunday real estate section of a local paper. People look for new houses on Sunday. Second best place is a real estate magazine. Most areas have at least one. There is one for every resort area and sometimes one for financially attractive sections of a large city. Look for informal advertising opportunities. I list my houses in the real estate file of a Bell Telephone operation in my vicinity. It hires hundreds of employees from out of town.

Intelligent Selling to Maximize the Recycle Profit 145

Pitching Prospects Face to Face

The carnival pitch-man who tries to entice you to buy a ticket to the side show isn't exactly the image you want to present, but you do have to make a pitch to intrigue people enough to come look at your place.

There is a thin line between truth and fiction here, and it is better to err on the truth side if there is a question in your mind. The "puffing" of real estate through half-truths is a time-honored tradition. But, if you have made a good recycle, you don't need to puff the place. Just tell it like it is. Should a new prospect go ahead with the purchase, there is at least a month's lapse to the final closing. If, in that time, the buyer finds out he was not given the straight facts, he may abandon the deal.

The Effect of the Entrance

The most important impression is the first impression: Buyers tend to stay with that. Dress up the front porch and the foyer, and you have half the battle won.

Place freshly cut flowers in the front hall, have the entrance well lit, and the air fresh smelling throughout the house. Have a fire in the fireplace, a fresh pot of coffee brewing on the stove, and rolls in the oven. Put up a good show, particulary the first few days. Sixty percent of the exposure will come in the first few days.

Even if you don't sell the house right away, keep the special touches going. I know of one place that did not sell for three months. Then, one cold day when the owner arrived to show the house, she built a fire in the fireplace to warm it up during the visit. Three sets of people came by that afternoon to see the house. Two bid on it. One bought it. The fire did the trick.

Setting Up the Meeting

There are two ways to meet a prospect: The first is to wait for the prospect to come to the house; the second is to meet him or her somewhere else.

The second gambit is often worthwhile if you have an expensive house to sell and you want to size the prospect up before you start putting valuable time into dealing with him.

Whether you meet the person at the house or elsewhere, you have to have vital facts and figures for the meeting well in hand: (1) the monthly mortgage installment, (2) the down payment amount, (3) mortgage availability, (4) the town tax per year, (5) the fuel bills per month. These are all figures of great interest to a prospect. If it is a family with children, they will want to know about schools, parks, playgrounds, and recreation advantages.

Take time to find out what the prospect does and what his background is. You may get a valuable clue to the kind of amenities that will make him interested. Also, it will help put the prospect at ease. Before the tour is over, sit the prospect down in the most pleasant location in the house and talk to him for five or ten minutes, if you can. This gives him a chance to see how it could be to actually live in the house. This is the time to come out with coffee and rolls.

Listing the House with Realty People

If you put energy into a good solid contact with a series of prospective buyers and find you do not like that kind of dealing, then consider hiring an agent and listing the house with a real estate agency. The advantages are easy to see:

1. You don't have to show the house yourself.
2. The agent takes care of qualifying the buyer and finding a mortgage.
3. The agent takes responsibility for being there at the convenience of the prospect.
4. The agent can be more convincing than a home owner.
5. The agent will advertise your place without cost to you.
6. The agent is the one who risks time and energy, not you.

That is quite a list of advantages. And, since the agent does this for a living, he will be good at all these things. Right? Not necessarily.

Agents and brokers are like any other class of professionals. You have to shop for the best.

If you want to get the best agents on your case, you interview the agents at their office and see if they seem on the ball. Also find out how much they advertise their properties. And check to see if their For Sale signs are all around town.

I always put my houses in "multiple listing." (You list with one agent asking for a multiple listing and that agent will put you on the list of all the agents in the area.) The more times the house is shown, the more likely it is to sell.

A good agent *can* really be a key to a sale. Through knowledge of the local real estate scene and the credibility that his expertise gives him, the agent can be a very persuasive voice on your behalf. If a broker tells a prospect, "This house is the best buy in town right now," it carries weight. A good broker is familiar with the school situation, the tax picture, the mortgage picture, and with comparative heating and electrical costs. The prospect *listens* to him.

Getting Them to Sign on the Line

A prospect is most likely to commit himself when he first sees the house. If he decides to buy, get the prospect to sign a "short form" contract of sale, specifying the location, price, and amount of earnest money changing hands. Legally the contract may not be binding (because it does not have enough detail to satisfy a court), but the buyer, having signed, is psychologically committed to going ahead. If he's willing to sign, he's "for real." And he is more likely to take the next step: signing the long-form standard contract of sale. (This document, as we have previously noted, spells out conditions for legal transfer of the title, such as the closing date, specific repairs to be made by you, and changes that you agree to make before closing date.)

The Follow-Up Period

A month or so usually elapses between the signing of the contract and the closing. In that time, you need to keep the house looking as good as it did when your buyer made his commitment. Keep the lawns mowed, the house heated, and the flowers blooming. This will reassure the prospect who may well come back time and again to look at the place he is buying.

He may want to show his friends and relatives, some of whom will try to point out the defects, if any are visible. So, if the buyer asks to see the house again, make sure that either you or your agent is present to counteract any negative comments by third parties on the scene. A new buyer is understandably jittery and will be susceptible to negative comments.

Another advantage to keeping the house looking its best is that if the contract of sale specifies plumbing and termite inspections, for instance, any inspector will look more favorably on a house that is carefully maintained than a house that is run-down and worn-out looking.

Finally the Closing

So, here it comes, the big moment. You have bought, recycled, and sold a house. You have made a good chunk of money out of it. Right there is the buyer's check. Your diploma.

You have taken a huge step forward in the race against inflation. You may be so far ahead that inflation will never again catch up with you. At the very least, you have taken out a good deal of the sting. And, if you choose, you can recycle a second house, for an even better profit and another giant step ahead. The skills and the attitude of the successful recycler will stand you in good stead, not only in business but in life.

Index

A

Accountant, need for, to handle finances, 75
Accounting system, setting up for, 74-75
Advertising, role of, in setting up presentation, 144
Aluminum ladders, 87
Appraisal, need for, for high-priced valuables, 76
Appraised value, dealing with low, in recycling, 40
Appreciation, and recycling, 22
Architects, role of, in house design, 66, 72-73
Attic, insulation of, 95

B

Balloon payments, 43-44, 141
Banks, convincing to back recycling ventures, 9-10
Basement, insulation of, 96-97
Bathroom, as big selling point, 137
Bids
   art and necessity of low, 32
   discipline of low, 34
   figuring of, 28-29, 49-51
   psychological side of low, 32-33
Boiler, replacement of, 111-12
Brick walls, inspecting for problems, 124-25
Building codes, and paperwork, 72-73
Building inspector, 74, 106
Building permits, obtaining of, 73
Building list, 73-74
Buyers
   qualification of, 138, 141-42
   scarcity of, and recycling, 9
Buying-recycling, as way to make money recycling, 30

C

Capital gains, taxing of, 13
Carpenter's apron, 89
Carpeting, installation of, 133-34
Cash flow, need for, in recycling, 35-36
Cathedral ceilings, 132
Ceiling tiles, 131
Ceilings, renovation of, 131-32

Ceramic tiles, use of, 136
Certificates of deposit, as an investment, 7
Check, paying for everything with, 74–75
Chimney, inspection of, 124
Circuit tester, 117
Circulating pump, addition of, to existing heating system, 113
Cleaning woman's special, 18–19
Closing, 51–55, 148
Coal, as heating fuel, 109
Color schemes, importance of, in recycling, 134–35
Common stock, as an investment, 7
Community development loan, 49
Construction loans, 47
Contract of sale, 51
Contracting out, 79
Contractor, serving as your own, to build up profit, 78–83
Contractor's loans, 48
Copper pipe, 102, 105
  joining of, 106
Creation, feelings of, and recycling, 15
Creative mortgages, 139, 141
Credit cards, 48
Curb appeal, 123

D

Disposal system, 103
Down payment, 35
Drain snake, use of, 104–5
Drain system, 102
  clogs in, 104–5
Draperies, coordinating of, with wallcoverings, 136

E

Earnest money, 51
Easements, 53
Eaves, looking under, 123
Electric grinding wheel, 89
Electrical work
  estimation of costs of, 115
  inspection of service panel, 114–15
  installation of new circuit, 119–20
  making diagram for, 116–17
  modernizing of, 114–16
  nature of accidents in, 117–18
  putting in new system, 116
  and safety, 115, 117–18
  as top-of-ladder job, 120
  use of house ground, 118–19
Electricity
  as heating fuel, 108, 109
  safety in use of, 87
Entrance, effect of, on prospects, 145
Equity, 39–40, 45–46
Escrow, 55
Exhaust fan, 66
Exterior changes
  deciding order of, 93–94
  gauging of, 64
  and judgment on what to do, 67–68
  making extensive, 64
  and the neighborhood standard, 65
  and painting, 125
  patching siding, 125
  nad redesign, 126–27
  restoring trim, 125
  and roofing, 123, 125–26

to bring in prospects, 123-28
versus interior changes, 63-64

F

Family loan, 48
Federal Housing Authority, as loan source, 49
Filters, replacement of in hot air heating systems, 112
First inpressions, importance of, 145
Fixed rate mortgage, 44
Flashing, looking at, 124
Flea markets
    as source for building materials, 82-83
    as source for cheap tools, 86
Floor tiles, installation of, 134
Floors, renovating of, 133-34
Foundation, inspecting for problems, 124-25

G

Garden pools, addition of, 128
Gloves, and use of tools, 88
Government-sponsored mortgages, 139-40
Ground fault interrupter (GFI), 87

H

Handyman's special, 18-19
Heat exchanger, replacement of, 111
Heat pumps, 110, 111
Heating systems
    fuels and carriers in, 107-8
    hot air systems, 108-9
    hot water carrier systems, 109
    inspection of existing, 111-12
    recycling of, 110
    replacement with new, 110-11
    steam, refrigerant, and radiant carriers, 109-10
    upgrading of existing, 112-13
Hiring contractors, as not always the answer, 80
Home improvement loans, 48
Home ownership
    and recycling, 5, 6-7, 9
Homework, doing of, and recycling, 22-23
Horizontal lines, use of, in decorating, 135
Hot air heating systems, 108-9
    advantages of, 110-11
Hot water carrier heating systems, 109
    advantages of, 111
House auctions, as source for cheap tools, 86
House Beautiful syndrome, 67
House ground, use of, 118-19
Houses, looking for ideal to recycle, 17-23
Housing and Urban Development (HUD), Department of, as loan source, 49
How We Made a Million Dollars Recycling Great Old Houses, 5

I

Incredible Illustrated Tool Book, 86
Inflation, 13

Insulation
  of attic, 95
  of the basement, 96-97
  cutting losses through siding, 98
  cutting losses through windows, 98-99
  doing it versus having it done, 95-96
  functions of, 94-95
  and the moisture problem, 96
  of the roof, 96-97
  types of, 95-96
  of the walls, 97-98
Insurance, need for, 76
Interest, as not a problem in short-term recycling, 8-9
Interior changes
  and adding space to old houses, 130-31
  of bathroom, 137
  color schemes for, 134-35
  deciding order of, 93-94
  and doing interior walls, 132-33
  and finishing of wood trim, 135-36
  and the *House Beautiful* syndrome, 67
  importance of structural wall, 66-67
  inspection for, 129
  and interior design of space, 130
  and judgment of what and what not to do, 67-68
  opening up of house, 66
  planning ideas for, 65-66
  and renovation of ceilings first, 131-32
  and renovation of floors, 133-34
  use of ceramic tiles in, 136
  use of mirrors in, 137
  use of wallcoverings in, 136
  using horizontal and vertical lines in, 135
  using paints for effect, 135
  versus exterior changes, 63-64
Investments, looking at, 5-7

J

Judgment
  need for, in recycling, 10-12
  on what changes to make in recycle house, 62-63, 67-68

K

Kitchen, as key to market price of house, 20

L

Ladder of needs, 17-19
Ladders, use of aluminum, 87
Landscaping, 128
Lawyers
  and need for paperwork in dealing with, 70-71
  need for, in real estate dealings, 51
  as source of mortgage information, 139
Life insurance loans, 48
Light, letting in, 127
Linoleum, installation of, 134
Location, as important in recycling, 22

M

Mansion recycles, 2
Materials, using good, 61-62
Middle-of-the-ladder recycles, 20-21
Mirrors, use of, to expand space, 137
Moldings, restoration of ceiling, 132
Money market funds, as an investment, 7
Mortgages
  becoming a good risk in, 41-42
  creative approaches to, 43-44, 141
  finding of
    for buyer, 138-42
    for recycle project, 35-44
  government sources for, 49
  kinds of, 139-40
  private sources for, 46-47
  and qualification of buyer, 141-42
  second, 45-46
  short-term financing sources, 47-48
  sources of information on, 36-37, 139
  take-back (owner), 46, 139, 140-41
  traditional bank, 37-39
  unusual sources for, 48-49
Multiple listings, 147
Mutual funds, as an investment, 7

N

Natural gas, as heating fuel, 108, 109

Negative speculation profit, 32
Neighborhood, as important in recycling, 22
Neighborhood standard, importance of meeting, 61
Nonunion work, versus union work, 81-82

O

Occupancy permit, need for, 73
Oil, as heating fuel, 108, 109
Older house, making space in, 130-31
Open-house color plans, 135
Opening up of house, 66
Organization, and use of tools, 88
Outbuildings, addition of, 127-28
Owner mortgages, 46, 139, 140-41

P

Painting
  of exterior, 125
  for interior effect, 135
Paneling, use of, for interior walls, 133
Paperwork, importance of, in recycling, 69-77
Partnership mortgage, 44
Passbook loans, 47-48
Passive solar heat, 108
Peninsula House, recycling of, 2-3, 14
Personal injury suits, insurance coverage for, 76
Pipe scale, clogging of hot water systems, 112
Planning board hearings, and paperwork, 71-72

Plastering, of ceilings, 132
Plastic glasses, and use of tools, 87–88
Plastic pipe, 101–2, 105
Plumber's helper, use of, 104
Plumbing
   adding or replacing pipes in, 105–6
   addition of new, 101
   drain problem spots in, 104–5
   inspection of, 101, 103–4
   joining copper piping, 106
   necessitites in, 100
   as three systems, 102–3
   types of materials to use, 101–2
   vent system in, 103, 105
Plumbing code, need for, 106
Presentation
   effect of entrance on, 145
   follow-up period, 148
   getting prospects to sign on the line, 147–48
   of house, 144
   listing of house with realty people, 146–47
   pitching prospects face to face, 145
   preparation for, 143–44
   role of advertising in, 144
   setting up meeting, 145–46
Pressure plumbing system, 102, 103–4
Private mortgage sources, 46–47
Private space, 130
Prospects
   getting signature of, on contract, 147–48
   pitching face to face, 145
   setting up meeting, 145–46
Public space, 130

Q

Qualification of buyer, 138, 141–42

R

R value of insulation, 95
Radiant heat, 110, 113
Real estate broker
   buying recyclable property through, 76–77
   listing recycled house with, 146–47
Real estate deed, 52–53
Recycle plan
   need for, 42
   using day-to-day, 80–81
Recycling
   as a positive experience, 15
   as a short-term process, 8
   and being willing, 13–15
   commitment to, 4
   goals of, 3
   heart of, 3–4
   importance of paperwork in, 69–77
   and judgment on what changes to make, 10–12, 62–63, 67–68
   in the 1980s, 5–7
   looking for ideal house for, 17–23
   making rough estimate in, 59–68
   nine steps to, 16
   payoffs of, 12–13
   rewards of, 1–3
   three ways of making money on, 29

buy-recycle, 31
rental, 29–30
speculation-recycle, 31–32
Redecorating vs. recycling, 3–4
Refrigerants, use of, in heat pump, 110
Remortgage gambit, 39–40
Rental options
and paperwork, 71
and recycling, 13, 29–30
Retaining walls, addition of, 128
Ridge beams, 97
Ridge line, looking at, 124
Right of way, 53
Risk capital, 48–49
Risk capital loan, 40
Rolling the loan over, 44, 47
Roof, insulation of, 96–97
Roofing, 78
inspection of, 123–24
replacement of, 126
restoration of, 125–26
Rough estimate, making of, 59–68
Running-out-of-gas trap, 61

S

Safety
and electricity, 115, 117–18
and use of tools, 86–88
Salvaging, in recycling, 82–83
Sand paints, using for effect, 135
Savings account, as an investment, 7
Second mortgage financing, 45–46
Shoestring trap, 61
Shopping around, for a recycle, 19–20
Short-term financing, 47–48
Siding, 127
cutting heat loss through, 98
patching of, 125
Solar heat, 108, 109, 111
Space, interior design of, 130
Speculation loss, 32
Speculation-recycling, as way to make money recycling, 6, 7, 9, 31–32
Steam heating systems, 109–11
upgrading of, 113
Structural wall, 66–67
Structuralite, 131
Stucco ceilings, 131
Stucco walls, inspecting for problems, 124–25
Subcontracting, 79
Subdivision rights, 48
Supplier's loans, 48
Sure-fire recycles, 27–34

T

Take-back (owner) mortgages, 46, 139, 140–41
Tax advantages, of recycling, 12–13
Telephone conversations, keeping records of, 70
Texture paint
for ceilings, 132
for effect, 133, 135
for rough walls, 62
Time-is-of-essence clause, 52
Title insurance, 53–54
Title I loan, 49
Title search, 53–54
Tools
buying on the cheap, 86
and efficiency, 89

for plumbing repairs, 102
maintenance of, 89–90
organization of, 88
safety in use of, 86–88
use of by recycler vs. home shop use, 84–85
wear and tear on, 85
Tools and Their Uses, 86
Top-of-the-ladder recycles, 20–21
electrical work as, 120
Traffic space, 130
Trim
adding of, 126–27
restoring of, 125

U

Union work, versus nonunion work, 81–82
Umbrella insurance, need for, 76

V

Vapor barrier, installation of proper side of, 96–97
Variable-rate mortgage, 44
Vent system, problems in, 105
Vents, installation of, in attic, 97

Vertical lines, use of, in decorating, 135
Veterans Administration, as loan source, 49
Victorian houses, as profitable to recycle, 21–22

W

Walking the line, 53
Wallpapering
of ceilings, 131–32
of interior walls, 132–33, 136
Walls, insulation of, 97–98
Weir limit, 28
Weir rule
figuring bid under, 49–51
for sure-fire recycle, 27–34
Window boxes, as trim, 126–27
Windows, cutting heat loss through, 98–99
Wood, as heating fuel, 109, 111
Wood trim, finishing coat for, 135–36

Z

Zoning, and paperwork, 71–72